greatest ever

party food

This is a Parragon Publishing Book
This edition published in 2006

Parragon Publishing
Queen Street House
4 Queen Street
Bath BA1 1HE, UK

Copyright © Parragon Books Ltd 2004

ISBN: 1-40543-116-4

Printed in Indonesia

Produced by the Bridgewater Book Company Ltd.

NOTE

This book uses imperial, metric, and US cup measurements. Follow the
same units of measurement throughout; do not mix imperial and metric.
All spoon measurements are level: teaspoons are assumed to be 5 ml,
and tablespoons are assumed to be 15 ml. Unless otherwise stated,
milk is assumed to be whole, eggs, and individual vegetables such as
potatoes are medium, and pepper is freshly ground black pepper.

The times given for each recipe are an approximate guide
only because the cooking times may vary as a result of the
types of oven and other equipment used.

Recipes using raw or very lightly cooked eggs should be avoided by infants,
the elderly, pregnant women, convalescents, and anyone suffering from an
illness. Pregnant and breastfeeding women are advised to avoid
eating peanuts and peanut products.

Contents

Introduction

Party food is the ideal option for sociable eating and entertaining in today's world. It fits perfectly with contemporary lifestyles, being relatively quick and easy to prepare, interesting, and stylish in appearance yet informal and fun to eat, not to mention light on the time and effort  involved in cleaning up after the event. It is also food that will give you pleasure in the making of it, in addition to the immense satisfaction you will experience when your guests show their appreciation of the end results. There is a wealth of recipe ideas in this book for you to choose from to prepare a range of delicious dishes for every kind of occasion, from a summer lunch party alfresco or a family picnic, to an old-style, sophisticated cocktail party or a celebratory evening event. Whatever the occasion, take time to plan ahead. Select recipes that are appropriate to your guests' tastes and that will work well in combination with one another, both in terms of flavor and appearance as well as demands on your time in preparation. On the day, you can then feel confident that your guests will enjoy each and every morsel and minute.

The recipes in this book encompass every kind of main ingredient and flavoring, including a wide range of vegetable and vegetarian options, so that there is something to suit all tastes.

All the popular cuisines are represented and all the classic party-food favorites from around the globe are featured, including Italian Bruschetta and Focaccia; French Tapenade and Quiche Lorraine; Chinese Egg Rolls and Dim Sum; Indian Samosas and Bhajis; Greek Tzatziki and Taramasalata; Middle Eastern Hummus and Baba Ghanoush; Mexican Guacamole and Nachos; Jewish Chopped Liver and Herring, not forgetting Traditional English Potted Shrimp and Sausage Rolls.

The emphasis of the book is very much on speed and ease, since while we all want our guests to enjoy the food, we don't want to spend so much time in the kitchen that we are too tired to enjoy the proceedings ourselves. However, much

thought has been given to creative presentation, so that even a simple dish will look impressive when served, with accompanying ideas and recipes for intriguing garnishes, sociable dipping sauces, and other condiments and interesting side servings.

Many of the dishes can be prepared in advance, such as those in the Dips & Spreads chapter (see pages 8–55). These can then be presented with a variety of specialty breads, cookies, or crackers, either store-bought or homemade. The Breads chapter (see pages 212–53) includes recipes for bread

sticks, cheese straws, and other tasty accompaniments.

There are many recipes for dishes that are delicious served cold, so that you can be relaxed about when to serve and also to cater for alfresco occasions, particularly picnics.

Even many of the nibbles best served hot can be prepared in advance and just popped in an oven or under the broiler to heat through when the time is right —and often being individually sized, this doesn't take long. This also gives you the opportunity to orchestrate eating in stages throughout the course of an occasion, serving different dishes at various intervals, rather than a range all at once. Again, this makes for a more relaxed atmosphere and encourages social interaction.

But bear in mind that these fabulous party-food dishes can be enjoyed any day of the week, with family for a lunch or brunch, or as a treat by yourself or to share with a friend or partner. Above all, this is food to savor and enjoy.

Entertaining Essentials

Hosting a party, and making some tempting nibbles for your guests, should be fun. All you need is a selection of recipes, and some careful preparation.

Party Basics

Don't forget that there are plenty of ready-made nibbles that you can buy to increase the variety of your party snacks. Plain and flavored bread sticks, corn and tortilla chips, as well as plain potato chips, are great for dunking into homemade dips or just for nibbling on their own. Peanuts are party favorites, but you can also include cashews, almonds, and pistachios. A selection of cheeses and a basket of crackers or crusty bread, served with a dish of butter, is easy and always popular.

If you are already planning to prepare a range of flavorsome foods, you can supplement them with some simpler snacks, such as broiled chicken drumsticks, sausages on sticks, and squares of toast with ready-made toppings such as lumpfish caviar, sliced hard-cooked eggs, smoked salmon, slices of salami, and soft cheese and chives. Garnish with fresh herb sprigs, sliced stuffed olives, pearl onions, or tiny gherkins. Sandwiches, however, are best avoided because they quickly dry out.

If you don't mind providing cutlery as well as plates, you can also serve a selection of salads. Most supermarkets sell a wide selection of mixed leaf and vegetable salads, which

are ideal. Pasta and rice salads with a colorful mixture of drained canned corn kernels, red and yellow bell pepper strips, tomato wedges, cooked frozen peas, and strips of ham are easily made and can be dressed with vinaigrette or mayonnaise.

Crudités
Raw and blanched vegetables are perfect for serving with most dips and look very tempting on a large serving platter. Seed and slice red, yellow, or orange bell peppers lengthwise. Baby corn cobs

and trimmed, thin asparagus should be blanched in lightly salted boiling water. Include whole cherry tomatoes, small white mushrooms, and trimmed radishes, perhaps with a few small leaves attached. Trim and separate the leaves of red and white chicory or the hearts of Boston lettuces. Cut raw cauliflower into small florets and slice carrots, celery, and cucumber into sticks.

Vegetable Chips
Homemade vegetable chips make a delicious alternative to ordinary potato chips. You can,

of course, use potatoes, but you might also like to try parsnips, carrots, or sweet potatoes. Peel the vegetables and slice very thinly using a mandoline or swivel-blade vegetable peeler. Heat corn or peanut oil in a deep-fat fryer or large pan to 350–375°F/ 180–190°C, or until a cube of bread browns in 30 seconds. Add the vegetable slices to the oil and deep-fry until golden. Drain thoroughly on paper towels and sprinkle with sea salt, paprika, or cayenne pepper. Store in an airtight container when cold.

Dips & Spreads

Dips and spreads are invariably quick and easy to make, and are also highly versatile. Ingredients are simply whizzed up in a food processor or just beaten together in a bowl to create such international favorites as Aïoli (see page 10), Hummus (see page 12), Taramasalata (see page 16), Guacamole (see page 18), and Hot Mexican Salsas (see page 32), to serve with crisp and colorful vegetable crudités, bread sticks, or tortilla chips for dunking. Other dishes are ideal for spreading lavishly onto hunks of bread, slices of Melba toast, or crackers, such as Tapenade (see page 20), Smoked Mackerel Pâté (see page 40), or Quick Chicken Liver Pâté (see page 42), for a lunch or supper get-together, or the first course of a special dinner. You can also pack little cartons into a picnic or lunch box for a delicious portable banquet. The possibilities are endless.

aïoli

serves eight

4 garlic cloves

2 egg yolks

1 cup olive oil

lemon juice

salt and pepper

TO SERVE

Crudités (see page 36)

8 hard-cooked eggs, shelled

1 Place the garlic cloves and a pinch of salt in a glass bowl and crush with the back of a spoon. Add the egg yolks and beat briefly with an electric mixer until creamy.

2 Add the oil, a few drops at a time, beating constantly with an electric mixer, until the mixture starts to thicken. Then add the remaining oil in a thin, steady stream, beating the mixture constantly.

3 Stir in a little lemon juice to give the mayonnaise a dipping consistency. Season to taste with a little more salt, if necessary, and pepper. Cover with plastic wrap and let chill in the refrigerator until required.

4 Before serving, return the aïoli to room temperature, if necessary, and transfer to a serving bowl. Arrange the Crudités on a large serving platter with the eggs and serve with the aïoli.

red bell pepper dip

serves eight

3 red bell peppers, halved
   and seeded

1 cup cream cheese or curd cheese

½ tsp cayenne pepper

salt

TO SERVE

cherry tomatoes

radishes

radicchio leaves

white mushrooms, halved

cauliflower florets

celery stalks

3 Stir in the cream cheese or curd cheese until smooth, then stir in the cayenne pepper and salt to taste. Cover with plastic wrap and let chill in the refrigerator until required.

4 To serve, place the bowl in the center of a large platter and arrange the tomatoes, radishes, radicchio, mushrooms, cauliflower, and celery around it.

1 Preheat the broiler. Arrange the bell pepper halves, skin-side up, on a baking sheet and place under the hot broiler for 10–15 minutes, or until the skins start to blacken and blister. Using tongs, transfer to a plastic bag, tie the top, and set aside until the bell peppers are cool enough to handle.

2 Remove the bell peppers from the bag and peel away the skins. Coarsely chop the flesh and place in a food processor. Process to a smooth purée, then scrape into a serving bowl.

hummus with lebanese seed bread

serves eight

12 oz/350 g canned chickpeas,
    rinsed and drained

1 cup sesame seed paste

4 garlic cloves

juice of 3 lemons

6 tbsp water

salt and pepper

2 tbsp olive oil

LEBANESE SEED BREAD

scant ⅓ cup toasted sesame seeds

½ cup poppy seeds

4 tbsp chopped fresh thyme

⅔ cup olive oil

6 pita breads

TO GARNISH

2 tbsp chopped fresh
    flatleaf parsley

cayenne pepper

black olives, to serve

1 Preheat the broiler. For the bread, place the seeds and thyme in a mortar and crush lightly with a pestle. Stir in the oil. Gently split open the pita breads and brush the seed mixture over the cut sides. Cook under the hot broiler until golden brown and crisp. Set aside to cool. Store the pitas in an airtight container until required.

2 Place the chickpeas, sesame seed paste, garlic, lemon juice and 4 tablespoons of the water in a food processor. Process until smooth, adding the remaining water if necessary. Alternatively, mash all the ingredients together in a bowl with a fork.

3 Spoon the mixture into a serving dish and season to taste with salt and pepper. Make a shallow hollow in the top of the hummus and spoon in the oil. If you are not serving it immediately, cover with plastic wrap and let chill until required.

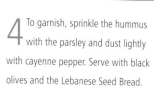

4 To garnish, sprinkle the hummus with the parsley and dust lightly with cayenne pepper. Serve with black olives and the Lebanese Seed Bread.

baba ghanoush

serves eight

3 large eggplants

3 garlic cloves, chopped

6 tbsp sesame seed paste

6 tbsp lemon juice

1 tsp ground cumin

3 tbsp chopped fresh flatleaf parsley

salt and pepper

fresh flatleaf parsley sprigs,
   to garnish

Vegetable Chips (see page 7),
   to serve

1 Preheat the broiler to low. Prick the eggplants all over with a fork and cut in half lengthwise. Arrange the halves, skin side up, on a baking sheet and place under the broiler for 15 minutes, or until the skins start to blacken and blister and the flesh feels soft. Remove from the broiler and set aside until cool enough to handle.

2 Peel the eggplants and squeeze out any excess moisture, then coarsely chop the flesh and place in a food processor. Add the garlic and 2 tablespoons of the sesame seed paste and process to mix, then add 2 tablespoons lemon juice and process again. Continue adding the sesame seed paste and lemon juice alternately, processing between each addition.

3 When the mixture is smooth, scrape it into a bowl and stir in the cumin and chopped parsley. Season to taste with salt and pepper.

4 Transfer the dip to a serving dish. If you are not serving it immediately, cover and let chill in the refrigerator until required. Return the dip to room temperature to serve. Garnish with parsley sprigs and serve with Vegetable Chips.

tzatziki

serves eight

1 cucumber

2 garlic cloves

8 scallions

2½ cups strained yogurt

5 tbsp chopped fresh mint, plus

    extra to garnish

salt and pepper

TO SERVE

toasted mini pita breads

Sesame Bread Sticks (see page 246)

1 Trim the cucumber, but do not peel. Cut the cucumber into small, neat dice. Finely chop the garlic and scallions.

2 Beat the yogurt in a bowl with a fork until smooth, then fold in the cucumber, garlic, scallions, and mint. Season the mixture to taste with salt and pepper.

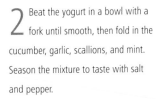

3 Transfer to a serving bowl, cover with plastic wrap, and let chill in the refrigerator until required. Serve the dip with toasted mini pita breads and Sesame Bread Sticks.

taramasalata

serves eight

8 oz/225 g stale white bread,
   crusts removed

12 oz/350 g smoked cod's roe

2 garlic cloves, chopped

2 slices onion

4 tbsp lemon juice

¾ cup olive oil

black kalamata olives, to garnish

chunks of crusty bread, to serve

1 Coarsely tear up the bread and place it in a bowl. Add cold water to cover and set aside to soak for 10 minutes.

2 Meanwhile, using a sharp knife, scrape the roe away from the thick, outer skin. Place the roe in a food processor with the garlic, onion, and lemon juice. Drain the bread, squeeze out the excess water with your hands, and add it to the food processor. Process the mixture for 2 minutes, or until smooth.

3 With the motor running, gradually add the oil through the feeder tube until the mixture is smooth and creamy. Scrape into a serving dish, cover with plastic wrap, and let chill in the refrigerator until required.

4 Garnish the taramasalata with the olives. Serve with chunks of crusty bread.

guacamole

serves eight

4 avocados

2 garlic cloves

4 scallions

3 fresh red chilies, seeded

2 red bell peppers, seeded

5 tbsp olive oil

juice of 1½ limes

salt

chopped fresh cilantro leaves,
    to garnish

tortilla chips, to serve

1 Cut the avocados in half
lengthwise and twist the halves
to separate. Remove and discard the
pits and scoop out the flesh into a
large bowl with a spoon. Coarsely
mash with a fork.

2 Finely chop the garlic, scallions,
chilies, and bell peppers, then stir
them into the mashed avocado. Add
4 tablespoons of the oil and the lime
juice, season to taste with salt, and stir
well to mix. If you prefer a smoother
dip, process all the ingredients
together in a food processor.

3 Transfer the guacamole to a
serving bowl. Drizzle the
remaining oil over the top, sprinkle
with the cilantro, and serve with
tortilla chips.

eggplant spread

serves six–eight

2 large eggplants

1 tomato

1 garlic clove, chopped

4 tbsp extra virgin olive oil

2 tbsp lemon juice

2 tbsp pine nuts, lightly toasted

salt and pepper

2 scallions, finely chopped

TO GARNISH

ground cumin

2 tbsp finely chopped fresh
   flatleaf parsley

1 Preheat the oven to 450°F/230°C. Prick the eggplants all over with a fork. Place them on a baking sheet and roast in the preheated oven for 20–25 minutes, or until very soft.

2 Use a folded dish towel to remove the eggplants from the baking sheet and let cool.

3 Place the tomato in a heatproof bowl, pour boiling water over to cover, and let stand for 30 seconds. Drain, then plunge into cold water to prevent it cooking. Peel the tomato, then cut in half and scoop out the seeds with a teaspoon. Finely dice the flesh and set aside.

4 Cut the cooled eggplants in half lengthwise. Scoop out the flesh with a spoon and transfer to a food processor. Add the garlic, oil, lemon juice, and pine nuts and season to taste with salt and pepper. Process until smooth. Alternatively, mash in a bowl with a fork.

5 Scrape the mixture into a bowl and stir in the scallions and diced tomato. Cover with plastic wrap and let chill for 30 minutes before serving.

6 Garnish the dip with a pinch of cumin and the finely chopped parsley, then serve.

tapenade

serves six

thin slices day-old
  French baguette (optional)
olive oil (optional)
fresh flatleaf parsley sprigs,
  to garnish
cucumber strips, to serve (optional)
BLACK OLIVE TAPENADE
1½ cups black niçoise olives in
  brine, rinsed and pitted
1 large garlic clove
2 tbsp walnut pieces
4 canned anchovies, drained
about ½ cup extra virgin olive oil
lemon juice, to taste
pepper
GREEN OLIVE TAPENADE
1½ cups green olives in brine,
  rinsed and pitted
4 canned anchovies, drained
4 tbsp blanched almonds
1 tbsp capers in brine or
  vinegar, rinsed
about ½ cup extra virgin olive oil
1½–3 tsp finely grated orange rind
pepper

1 To make the Black Olive Tapenade, put the olives, garlic, walnut pieces, and anchovies in a food processor and process until blended.

2 With the motor running, slowly add the oil through the feeder tube, as if making mayonnaise. Add lemon juice and pepper to taste. Transfer the mixture to a bowl, cover with plastic wrap, and let chill in the refrigerator until required.

3 To make the Green Olive Tapenade, put the olives, anchovies, almonds, and capers in a food processor and process until blended. With the motor running, slowly add the oil through the feeder tube, as if making mayonnaise. Add orange rind and pepper to taste. Transfer the mixture to a bowl, cover with plastic wrap, and let chill in the refrigerator until required.

4 To serve on croûtes, if wished, toast the slices of bread on both sides until crisp. Brush 1 side of each slice with a little oil while they are still hot, so that the oil is absorbed.

5 Spread the croûtes with the tapenade of your choice and garnish with parsley. Alternatively, serve on cucumber strips.

vegetable cream dip

serves four

1 cup cream cheese

½ cup plain yogurt or sour cream

1 tbsp finely chopped fresh parsley

1 tbsp finely chopped fresh thyme

2 scallions, finely chopped

1 Beat the cream cheese in a large mixing bowl until it is soft and smooth.

2 Add the yogurt or sour cream, herbs and 1 scallion. Mix together well.

3 Cover with plastic wrap and let chill in the refrigerator for at least 30 minutes. Stir thoroughly before transferring to a serving dish.

4 Sprinkle the remaining scallion over the top of the dip to garnish before serving.

skordalia

serves six

2 oz/55 g day-old bread

½ cup almonds

4–6 large garlic cloves,
    coarsely chopped

⅔ cup extra virgin olive oil

2 tbsp white wine vinegar

salt and pepper

fresh flatleaf parsley or cilantro
    sprigs, to garnish

Sesame Bread Sticks (see page 246),
    to serve

VARIATION

Many versions of this rustic sauce
exist. For variety, replace the
bread with 4 tablespoons of
well-drained canned cannellini or
fava beans. You can replace the
white wine vinegar with freshly
squeezed lemon juice.

1 Cut the crusts off the bread and tear the bread into small pieces. Put in a bowl, pour over enough water to cover, and set aside to soak for 10–15 minutes. Squeeze the bread dry, then set aside.

2 To blanch the almonds, put them in a heatproof bowl and pour over just enough boiling water to cover. Let stand for 30 seconds, then drain. The skins should slide off easily.

3 Transfer the almonds and garlic to a food processor and process until finely chopped. Add the squeezed bread and process the mixture again until well blended.

4 With the motor running, gradually add the oil through the feeder tube in a thin, steady stream until a thick paste forms. Add the vinegar and process again. Season to taste with salt and pepper.

5 Scrape the mixture into a bowl, cover, and let chill until required. It will keep in the refrigerator for up to 4 days. To serve, garnish with herb sprigs. Serve with Sesame Bread Sticks.

vegetables with sesame dip

serves four

8 oz/225 g small broccoli florets

8 oz/225 g small cauliflower florets

8 oz/225 g asparagus, sliced
   into 2-inch/5-cm lengths

2 small red onions, cut into fourths

1 tbsp lime juice

2 tsp toasted sesame seeds

1 tbsp snipped fresh chives,
   to garnish

HOT SESAME & GARLIC DIP

1 tsp corn oil

2 garlic cloves, crushed

½–1 tsp chili powder

salt and pepper

2 tsp sesame seed paste

scant ¾ cup lowfat plain yogurt

2 tbsp snipped fresh chives

1 Line the base of a bamboo steamer with parchment paper and arrange the broccoli and cauliflower florets, asparagus, and onions on top.

2 Bring a wok or large pan of water to a boil and place the steamer on top. Sprinkle the vegetables with lime juice and steam for 10 minutes, or until they are just tender.

3 To make the Hot Sesame & Garlic Dip, heat the oil in a small, nonstick pan, add the garlic, chili powder, and salt and pepper to taste and cook gently for 2–3 minutes, or until the garlic is soft.

4 Remove the pan from the heat and stir in the sesame seed paste and lowfat plain yogurt. Return the pan to the heat and cook for 1–2 minutes without bringing to a boil. Stir in the chives.

5 Remove the vegetables from the steamer and place on a warmed serving platter. Sprinkle them with the sesame seeds and garnish with snipped chives. Serve with the Hot Sesame & Garlic Dip.

easy onion dip

serves four

1 cup sour cream

3 tbsp dried onion flakes

2 beef bouillon cubes, crumbled

COOK'S TIP

Stir in some chopped fresh herbs
before serving, such as parsley or
chives, and dust with paprika.

1 Combine the ingredients in a
small bowl and mix very well.

2 Cover with plastic wrap and let
chill for at least 30 minutes.

3 Stir thoroughly before transferring
to a serving dish.

buttered nut & lentil dip

serves four

4 tbsp butter

1 small onion, chopped

scant ½ cup split red lentils

1¼ cups vegetable stock

scant ½ cup blanched almonds

scant ½ cup pine nuts

½ tsp ground coriander

½ tsp ground cumin

½ tsp grated fresh gingerroot

1 tsp chopped fresh cilantro

salt and pepper

fresh cilantro sprigs, to garnish

TO SERVE

fresh vegetable Crudités

(see page 36)

bread sticks

VARIATION

Green or brown lentils can be used, but they will take longer to cook than red lentils. If you prefer, substitute peanuts for the almonds. Ground ginger can be used instead of fresh—substitute ½ teaspoon and add it with the other spices.

1 Melt half the butter in a pan, add the onion, and cook over medium heat, stirring frequently, until golden brown.

2 Add the lentils and stock. Bring to a boil, then reduce the heat and let simmer gently, uncovered, for 25–30 minutes, or until the lentils are tender. Drain well.

3 Melt the remaining butter in a small skillet. Add the almonds and pine nuts and cook over low heat, stirring frequently, until golden brown. Remove the skillet from the heat.

4 Put the lentils, almonds, and pine nuts in a food processor with any butter remaining in the skillet. Add the ground coriander, cumin, ginger, and chopped cilantro. Process for 15–20 seconds, until the mixture is smooth. Alternatively, press the lentils through a strainer with the back of a wooden spoon to purée them and then mix with the nuts, finely chopped, spices, and herbs.

5 Season the dip to taste with salt and pepper and garnish with cilantro sprigs. Serve with fresh vegetable Crudités and bread sticks.

heavenly garlic dip

serves four

2 garlic bulbs

6 tbsp olive oil

1 small onion, finely chopped

2 tbsp lemon juice

3 tbsp sesame seed paste

2 tbsp chopped fresh parsley

salt and pepper

fresh parsley sprigs, to garnish

fresh vegetable Crudités (see
　　page 36), French bread, or
　　warmed pita breads, to serve

VARIATION

If you come across smoked
garlic, use it in this recipe—it
tastes wonderful. There is no
need to roast the smoked garlic,
so omit the first step. This dip
can also be used to baste
vegetarian burgers.

1　Preheat the oven to 400°F/200°C.
Separate the bulbs of garlic into
individual cloves. Place them on
a baking sheet and roast in the
preheated oven for 8–10 minutes. Set
them aside to cool for a few minutes.

2　When they are cool enough to
handle, peel the garlic cloves,
then chop them finely.

3　Heat the oil in a pan or skillet and
add the garlic and onion. Cook
over low heat, stirring occasionally, for
8–10 minutes, or until soft. Remove
the pan from the heat.

4　Mix in the lemon juice, sesame
seed paste, and parsley. Season
with salt and pepper. Transfer the dip
to a heatproof bowl and keep warm.

5　Garnish with parsley sprigs and
serve with fresh vegetable
Crudités, or with chunks of French
bread, or warm pita breads.

sesame eggplant dip

serves four

1 eggplant

4–6 tbsp olive oil

juice of 1–2 lemons

4–6 tbsp sesame seed paste

1–2 garlic cloves, crushed

1 tsp sesame seeds, to garnish

1 Preheat a grill pan or broiler. Place the eggplant on the hot grill pan or under the broiler and cook, turning frequently, until the skin is blackened and blistered. The eggplant should be very soft.

2 Transfer to a cutting board and let cool slightly. Cut in half and scoop out the inside into a bowl. Mash with a fork to make a coarse paste.

3 Gradually add the oil, lemon juice, sesame seed paste and garlic. Mix well, tasting until you achieve the flavor and texture you like.

4 Transfer the mixture to a serving bowl and serve at room temperature. If not using immediately, cover with plastic wrap and let chill until 30 minutes before you need it.

5 Just before serving, toss the sesame seeds in a very hot, dry skillet for a few seconds to toast them. Sprinkle over the eggplant spread to garnish.

mint & cannellini bean dip

serves six

1 cup dried cannellini beans

1 small garlic clove, crushed

1 bunch scallions, coarsely chopped

handful of fresh mint leaves

2 tbsp sesame seed paste

2 tbsp olive oil

1 tsp ground cumin

1 tsp ground coriander

lemon juice

salt and pepper

fresh mint sprigs, to garnish

TO SERVE

fresh vegetable crudités, such as
 cauliflower florets, carrots,
 cucumber, radishes, and
 bell peppers

1 Put the cannellini beans in a bowl and then add enough cold water to cover. Set them aside to soak for at least 4 hours or overnight.

2 Rinse and drain the beans, put them into a large pan, and cover them with cold water. Bring to a boil, then boil rapidly for 10 minutes. Reduce the heat, cover, and let simmer until tender.

3 Drain the beans thoroughly and transfer them to a bowl or food processor. Add the garlic, scallions, mint, sesame seed paste, and olive oil. Process the mixture for about 15 seconds or mash well by hand until it is smooth.

4 Scrape the mixture into a bowl, if necessary, then stir in the cumin, coriander, and lemon juice to taste. Season to taste with salt and pepper. Mix thoroughly, cover with plastic wrap, and set aside in a cool place, but not the refrigerator, for 30 minutes to let the flavors develop.

5 Spoon the dip into individual serving bowls and garnish with sprigs of fresh mint. Place the bowls on plates and surround them with vegetable crudités. Serve the dip at room temperature.

hot mexican salsas

TROPICAL FRUIT SALSA

½ sweet ripe pineapple, peeled,
  cored, and diced

1 mango or papaya, seeded,
  peeled, and diced

½–1 fresh green chili, such as
  jalapeño or serrano, seeded
  and chopped

½–1 fresh red chili, chopped

½ red onion, chopped

1 tbsp sugar

juice of 1 lime

3 tbsp chopped fresh mint

salt

1 To make the Tropical Fruit Salsa,
  combine all the ingredients in a
large, nonmetallic bowl, adding salt to
taste. Cover the bowl and let chill in
the refrigerator until required.

2 For the Scorched Chili Salsa, char
  the bell pepper and chilies in a
dry skillet. Cool, peel, seed, and chop.
Mix with the garlic, lime juice, salt, and
oil in a nonmetallic bowl. Top with
oregano and cumin.

3 For the Salsa Verde, combine all
  the ingredients in a nonmetallic
bowl, adding salt to taste. If a
smoother sauce is preferred, process
the ingredients in a food processor
until blended. Spoon into a bowl
to serve.

SCORCHED CHILI SALSA

1 green bell pepper

2–3 fresh green chilies, such as
  jalapeño or serrano

2 garlic cloves, finely chopped

juice of ½ lime

1 tsp salt

2–3 tbsp extra virgin olive oil or
  vegetable oil

large pinch of dried oregano

large pinch of ground cumin

SALSA VERDE

1 lb/450 g canned tomatillos,
  drained and chopped, or tart
  fresh tomatoes, chopped

1–2 fresh green chilies, such as
  jalapeño or serrano, seeded and
  finely chopped

1 green bell pepper or large mild
  green chili, such as Anaheim or
  poblano, seeded and chopped

1 small onion, chopped

1 bunch fresh cilantro, finely
  chopped

½ tsp ground cumin

salt

chipotle salsa

makes about 2 cups

1 lb/450 g ripe juicy
   tomatoes, diced

3–5 garlic cloves, finely chopped

½ bunch fresh cilantro,
   coarsely chopped

1 small onion, chopped

1–2 tsp adobo marinade from
   canned chipotle chilies

½–1 tsp sugar

lime juice, to taste

salt

pinch of ground cinnamon
   (optional)

pinch of ground allspice (optional)

pinch of ground cumin (optional)

COOK'S TIP
To simplify preparation, the
fresh tomatoes can be replaced
with 14 oz/400 g canned
chopped tomatoes.

1 Place the diced tomatoes,
chopped garlic, and cilantro in
a food processor.

2 Process the mixture until smooth,
then add the onion, adobo
marinade, and sugar.

3 Squeeze in lime juice to taste.
Season to taste with salt, then
add the cinnamon, allspice, and cumin,
if using.

4 Serve at once, or cover and let
chill in the refrigerator until ready
to serve, although the salsa is at its
best when served freshly made.

hot salsa nachos

serves four

1–2 fresh jalapeño chilies

2 packs nachos or tortilla chips

4 oz/115 g Cheddar cheese, grated

2 tbsp finely chopped fresh cilantro,
   to garnish

TO SERVE

tomato salsa

Guacamole (see page 18)

sour cream

COOK'S TIP

If you cannot find fresh jalapeño
chilies, look out for ready-sliced
preserved jalapeño chilies in jars,
available from large
supermarkets.

1 Preheat the oven to 375°F/
190°C. Cut the chilies into
thin slices.

2 Tip the nachos or tortilla chips
into a shallow, ovenproof dish.
Sprinkle with the chili slices and top
with the cheese. Bake in the preheated
oven for 5–10 minutes, or until the
cheese is melting.

3 Remove from the oven, garnish
with cilantro, and serve with
tomato salsa, Guacamole, and a dish
of sour cream.

bagna cauda with crudités

serves eight

1 yellow bell pepper

3 celery stalks

2 carrots

4 oz/115 g mushrooms

½ cauliflower

1 fennel bulb

1 bunch scallions

2 beet, cooked and peeled

8 radishes

8 oz/225 g boiled new potatoes

1 cup olive oil

5 garlic cloves, crushed

1¾ oz/50 g canned anchovies in oil,
   drained and chopped

4 oz/115 g butter

Italian bread, to serve

1 Prepare the vegetables. Seed and thickly slice the bell pepper. Cut the celery into 3-inch/7.5-cm lengths. Cut the carrots into thin sticks. Score the mushrooms as in the main photograph. Separate the cauliflower into florets. Cut the fennel in half lengthwise, then cut each half into 4 lengthwise. Trim the scallions. Cut the beet into eighths. Trim the radishes. Cut the potatoes in half, if large. Arrange the prepared vegetables on a large serving platter.

COOK'S TIP

If you have one, a fondue set
is perfect for serving this dish
because the sauce can be kept
hot at the table.

2 Heat the oil very gently in a pan. Add the garlic and anchovies and cook very gently, stirring, until the anchovies have thoroughly mixed in. Take care not to brown or burn the garlic.

3 Add the butter and as soon as it has melted, serve at once with the selection of crudités and plenty of Italian bread.

crudités with shrimp sauce

serves four

about 1 lb 10 oz/750 g prepared
   raw fruit and vegetables, such
   as broccoli, cauliflower, apple,
   pineapple, cucumber, celery, bell
   peppers, and mushrooms

SAUCE

2¼ oz/60 g dried shrimp

½-inch/1-cm cube shrimp paste

3 garlic cloves, crushed

4 fresh red chilies, seeded
   and chopped

6 fresh cilantro sprigs,
   coarsely chopped

juice of 2 limes

Thai fish sauce, to taste

brown sugar, to taste

1 To make the sauce, put the dried shrimp in a bowl of warm water and soak for 10 minutes, then drain.

2 Place the shrimp paste, drained shrimp, garlic, chilies, and cilantro in a food processor and process until well chopped but not smooth.

3 Turn the sauce mixture into a bowl and add the lime juice, mixing well.

COOK'S TIP

Hard-cooked quail's eggs can be
added to this traditional fruit and
vegetable platter to create a dish
for a special occasion.

4 Add fish sauce and sugar to taste, then mix well.

5 Cover the bowl tightly and let chill in the refrigerator for at least 8 hours or overnight.

6 To serve, arrange the fruit and vegetables attractively on a large serving plate. Place the prepared sauce in the center for dipping.

eggplant dipping platter

serves four

1 eggplant, peeled and cut into
    1-inch/2.5-cm cubes

3 tbsp sesame seeds, roasted in a
    dry skillet over low heat

1 tsp sesame oil

grated rind and juice of ½ lime

1 small shallot, diced

1 tsp sugar

1 fresh red chili, seeded
    and sliced

salt and pepper

4 oz/115 g broccoli florets

2 carrots, cut into thin sticks

8 baby corn, cut in half lengthwise

2 celery stalks, cut into thin sticks

1 baby red cabbage, cut into
    8 wedges, the leaves of each
    wedge held together by the core

VARIATION

You can vary the selection of
vegetables depending on your
preference or whatever you have
at hand. Other vegetables you
could use are cauliflower florets
and thin cucumber sticks.

1 Bring a pan of water to a boil over medium heat. Add the eggplant and cook for 7–8 minutes. Drain well and let cool slightly.

2 Meanwhile, grind the sesame seeds with the oil in a food processor or in a mortar with a pestle.

3 Add the eggplant, lime rind and juice, shallot, sugar, and chili to the sesame seeds. Season to taste with salt and pepper, then process until smooth. Alternatively, chop and mash with a potato masher.

4 Adjust the seasoning to taste, then spoon the dip into a bowl.

5 Serve the dip surrounded by the prepared broccoli, carrots, baby corn, celery, and red cabbage.

smoked mackerel pâté

serves four

12 oz/350 g smoked mackerel,
  skinned and boned

6 oz/175 g butter, melted

½ cup heavy cream

3 tbsp lemon juice

salt and pepper

pinch of cayenne pepper

1 Put the fish into a food processor and blend with half the melted butter to a smooth paste.

2 Transfer the mixture to a bowl and gradually add the remaining butter with the cream and lemon juice. Season to taste with salt and pepper.

3 Spoon into a serving dish and sprinkle with cayenne pepper.

4 Cover with plastic wrap and chill for at least 1 hour before serving.

kipper pâté

serves eight

2 lb/900 g undyed kipper fillets

2 garlic cloves, finely chopped

¾ cup olive oil

6 tbsp light cream

salt and pepper

lemon slices, to garnish

oatcakes or crackers, to serve

1 Place the kippers in a large skillet or fish poacher and add cold water to just cover. Bring to a boil, then immediately reduce the heat and poach gently for 10 minutes until tender. If using a skillet, you may need to do this in batches.

2 Using a spatula, transfer the fish to a cutting board. Remove and discard the skin. Coarsely flake the flesh with a fork and remove any remaining tiny bones. Transfer the fish to a pan and add the garlic. Place over low heat and break up the fish with a wooden spoon.

3 Gradually add the oil, beating well after each addition. Add the cream and beat until smooth, but do not allow the mixture to boil.

4 Remove the pan from the heat and season to taste with salt, if necessary, and pepper. Spoon the pâté into serving dishes, cover, and set aside to cool completely. Let chill in the refrigerator until required (it can be refrigerated for up to 3 days).

5 Garnish with lemon slices and serve with oatcakes or crackers.

quick chicken liver pâté with melba toast

serves eight

2 tbsp olive oil

2 onions, chopped

2 garlic cloves, finely chopped

1 lb 8 oz/675 g chicken livers

3 tbsp brandy

2 tbsp chopped fresh parsley

1 tbsp chopped fresh sage

salt and pepper

scant 1⅓ cups cream cheese

fresh parsley sprigs, to garnish

MELBA TOAST

8 slices medium-thick white bread

1 Heat the oil in a large, heavy-bottom skillet over low heat. Add the onions and garlic and cook, stirring occasionally, for 5 minutes, or until softened.

2 Add the livers and cook, stirring and turning occasionally, for 5 minutes, or until they are lightly browned. Remove the skillet from the heat, stir in the brandy, parsley, and sage, and season to taste with salt and pepper. Let cool slightly.

3 Transfer the mixture to a food processor and process until smooth. You may need to scrape down the sides of the mixing bowl once or twice. Scrape the mixture into a bowl, cover with plastic wrap, and set aside to cool completely.

4 Meanwhile, for the Melba Toast, preheat the broiler to medium. Lightly toast the bread on both sides under the hot broiler. Cut off and discard the crusts, then cut each slice to make 2 very thin slices, each with 1 untoasted side. Toast the uncooked sides of the bread until the edges start to curl. Remove from the broiler and let cool. When completely cool, store in an airtight container until required.

5 When the chicken liver mixture is cold, stir in the cream cheese until thoroughly combined. Cover with plastic wrap and let chill in the refrigerator until required, but bring back to room temperature to serve. Garnish with parsley sprigs and serve with the Melba Toast.

parsley, chicken & ham pâté

serves four

8 oz/225 g skinless, boneless
   chicken, cooked
3½ oz/100 g lean ham
small bunch fresh parsley
1 tsp grated lime rind, plus extra
   to garnish
2 tbsp lime juice
1 garlic clove, peeled
generous ½ cup lowfat plain yogurt
salt and pepper
TO SERVE
lime wedges
crispbread or Melba Toast
   (see page 42)
salad greens

VARIATION

This pâté can be made
successfully with other kinds of
ground lean cooked meat, such
as turkey, beef, and pork.
Alternatively, replace the meat
with cooked shelled shrimp
and/or white crabmeat, or with
canned tuna in brine, drained.

1 Coarsely dice the chicken. Trim off and discard any fat from the ham and dice the meat. Place the chicken and ham in a food processor.

2 Add the parsley, lime rind and juice, and garlic and process until finely ground. Alternatively, finely chop the chicken, ham, parsley, and garlic and place in a bowl. Gently stir in the lime rind and juice.

3 Transfer the mixture to a bowl and stir in the lowfat plain yogurt. Season to taste with salt and pepper, cover with plastic wrap, and let chill in the refrigerator for 30 minutes.

4 Spoon the pâté into individual serving dishes and garnish with extra grated lime rind. Serve the pâté with lime wedges, crispbread, or Melba Toast and salad greens.

potato & bean pâté

serves four

3½ oz/100 g mealy potatoes, diced

8 oz/225 g mixed canned beans,

    such as cranberry, flageolet, and

    kidney beans, drained

1 garlic clove, crushed

2 tsp lime juice

1 tbsp chopped fresh cilantro,

    plus extra to garnish

salt and pepper

2 tbsp plain yogurt

COOK'S TIP

Serve on slices of homemade
Melba Toast (see page 42) or
use the store-bought variety
to save time and effort.
Alternatively, serve with Crudités
(see page 36). The pâté can
be stored for up to 2 days in
the refrigerator.

1 Cook the potatoes in a pan of boiling water for 10 minutes until tender. Drain well and mash.

2 Transfer the potato to a food processor and add the beans, garlic, lime juice, and cilantro. Season to taste with salt and pepper and process for 1 minute to make a smooth purée. Alternatively, mix the beans with the potato, garlic, lime juice, and cilantro and mash well.

3 Turn the purée into a bowl and add the yogurt. Mix together thoroughly.

4 Spoon the pâté into a serving dish. Serve at once, garnished with chopped cilantro, or cover with plastic wrap and let chill in the refrigerator until required.

cheese, garlic & herb pâté

serves four

1 tbsp butter

1 garlic clove, crushed

3 scallions, finely chopped

generous ½ cup fullfat cream cheese

2 tbsp chopped fresh mixed herbs,
    such as parsley, chives,
    marjoram, oregano, and basil

6 oz/175 g sharp Cheddar cheese,
    finely grated

4–6 slices white bread from a
    medium-cut sliced loaf

mixed salad greens and cherry
    tomatoes, to serve

TO GARNISH

ground paprika

fresh herb sprigs

1 Melt the butter in a small skillet over low heat. Add the garlic and scallions and cook for 3–4 minutes, or until softened. Let cool.

2 Beat the cream cheese in a large mixing bowl until smooth, then add the garlic and scallions. Stir in the chopped herbs, mixing well.

3 Add the cheese and work the mixture together to form a stiff paste. Cover and let chill in the refrigerator until ready to serve.

4 Toast the slices of bread on both sides, then cut off the crusts. Using a sharp bread knife, cut through the slices horizontally to make very thin slices. Cut into triangles and then lightly toast the untoasted sides until golden brown.

5 Arrange the mixed salad greens on 4 serving plates with the cherry tomatoes. Pile the pâté on top and sprinkle with a little paprika. Garnish with herb sprigs and serve with the toast triangles.

lentil pâté

serves four

1 tbsp vegetable oil, plus extra
   for oiling

1 onion, chopped

2 garlic cloves, crushed

1 tsp garam masala

½ tsp ground coriander

3½ cups vegetable stock

scant 1 cup split red lentils, rinsed

1 small egg

2 tbsp milk

2 tbsp mango chutney

2 tbsp chopped fresh parsley, plus
   extra to garnish

TO SERVE

salad greens

warm toast

VARIATION

Use other spices, such as chili powder or Chinese five-spice powder, to flavor the pâté and add tomato relish or chili relish instead of the mango chutney, if you prefer.

1 Preheat the oven to 400°F/ 200°C. Oil and line the bottom of a 1-lb/450-g loaf pan. Heat the oil in a large pan. Add the onion and garlic and cook for 2–3 minutes, stirring. Add the spices and cook for an additional 30 seconds.

2 Stir in the stock and lentils and bring the mixture to a boil. Reduce the heat and let simmer for 20 minutes, or until the lentils are tender and cooked. Remove the pan from the heat and drain off any excess moisture.

3 Place the mixture in a food processor and add the egg, milk, chutney, and parsley. Process the mixture until smooth.

4 Spoon the mixture into the prepared pan, smoothing the surface. Cover and cook in the preheated oven for 40–45 minutes, or until firm to the touch.

5 Let the pâté cool in the pan for 20 minutes, then transfer to the refrigerator to cool completely.

6 Turn out the pâté onto a serving plate, slice, and garnish with chopped parsley. Serve with salad greens and warm toast.

mushroom & chestnut pâté

serves eight

8 oz/225 g dried chestnuts,
   soaked overnight
¼ cup dried porcini mushrooms
4 tbsp hot water
4 tbsp Marsala or medium sherry
1 tbsp olive oil
1 lb 8 oz/675 g cremini
   mushrooms, sliced
1 tbsp balsamic vinegar
1 tbsp chopped fresh parsley
1 tbsp soy sauce
salt and pepper
thinly sliced radish, to garnish
whole-wheat toast triangles or
   crusty bread, to serve

1 Drain the chestnuts, place them in a pan, and add cold water to cover. Bring to a boil, then reduce the heat, cover, and let simmer for 45 minutes, or until tender. Drain well and set aside to cool.

2 Meanwhile, place the porcini mushrooms in a bowl with the hot water and 1 tablespoon of Marsala. Set aside to soak for 20 minutes. Drain well, reserving the soaking liquid. Pat the mushrooms dry with paper towels. Strain the soaking liquid through a fine strainer or coffee filter paper.

3 Heat the oil in a large, heavy-bottom skillet. Add the cremini mushrooms and cook over low heat, stirring occasionally, for 5 minutes, or until softened.

4 Add the porcini mushrooms, the reserved soaking liquid, and the vinegar. Cook, stirring constantly, for 1 minute. Increase the heat and stir in the remaining Marsala. Cook, stirring frequently, for 3 minutes. Remove the skillet from the heat.

5 Transfer the chestnuts to a food processor and process to a purée. Add the mushroom mixture and parsley and process to a smooth paste. Add the soy sauce and salt and pepper to taste and briefly process again to mix together.

6 Scrape the pâté into a serving bowl, cover, and let chill in the refrigerator. Garnish with radish slices before serving with toast triangles or crusty bread.

walnut, egg & cheese pâté

serves four

1 celery stalk

1–2 scallions

scant ¼ cup shelled walnuts

1 tbsp chopped fresh parsley

1 tsp chopped fresh dill or

⅓ tsp dried dill

1 garlic clove, crushed

dash of Worcestershire sauce

½ cup cottage cheese

2 oz/55 g blue cheese, such as

Stilton or Danablu

1 hard-cooked egg, shelled

salt and pepper

2 tbsp butter

fresh herbs, to garnish

crackers, toast, or crusty bread and

Crudités (see page 36), to serve

COOK'S TIP

You can also use this as a stuffing for vegetables. Cut the tops off large tomatoes, scoop out the seeds and fill with the pâté, piling it well up, or spoon into the hollows of celery stalks cut into 2-inch/5-cm pieces.

1 Finely chop the celery, slice the scallions very thinly, and chop the walnuts. Place in a bowl.

2 Add the herbs and garlic and Worcestershire sauce to taste. Mix well, then stir the cottage cheese evenly through the mixture.

3 Grate the blue cheese finely into the pâté mixture. Finely chop the hard-cooked egg and stir it into the mixture. Season to taste with salt and pepper.

4 Melt the butter and stir it into the pâté, then spoon into 1 serving dish or 4 individual dishes. Smooth the top, but do not press down firmly. Cover and let chill in the refrigerator until set.

5 Garnish with herbs and serve with crackers, toast, or fresh, crusty bread and a few Crudités.

black olive pâté

serves four

1⅓ cups pitted juicy black olives

1 garlic clove, crushed

finely grated rind of 1 lemon

4 tbsp lemon juice

½ cup fresh bread crumbs

¼ cup fullfat cream cheese

salt and pepper

lemon wedges, to garnish

TO SERVE

thick slices bread

mixture of olive oil and butter

1 Coarsely chop the olives and mix with the garlic, lemon rind and juice, bread crumbs, and cream cheese in a bowl. Pound the mixture in a mortar with a pestle until smooth, or place in a food processor and work until fully blended. Season to taste with salt and pepper.

2 Store the pâté in a screw-top jar and let chill for several hours before using—this allows the flavors to develop.

3 For a delicious cocktail snack, use a cookie cutter to cut out small circles from a thickly sliced loaf.

4 Heat oil and butter in a skillet, add the bread circles and cook until golden. Remove with a slotted spoon and drain well on paper towels.

5 Top each cooked bread circle with a little of the pâté, garnish with lemon wedges, and serve at once. This pâté will keep in an airtight jar in the refrigerator for up to 2 weeks.

tuna & anchovy pâté

serves six

1 3/4 oz/50 g canned anchovies,
    drained
14 oz/400 g canned tuna in
    brine, drained
3/4 cup lowfat cottage cheese
generous 1/2 cup skim milk
    soft cheese
1 tbsp horseradish relish
1/2 tsp grated orange rind
white pepper
4 thick slices whole-wheat bread
TO GARNISH
orange slices
fresh dill sprigs

1 Separate the anchovies and pat
well with paper towels to remove
all traces of oil.

2 Put the anchovies, tuna, cheeses,
horseradish relish, and orange
rind in a blender or food processor.
Season with white pepper and process
for a few seconds until smooth.
Alternatively, finely chop the anchovies
and flake the tuna, then beat together
with the other ingredients—this will
make a more textured pâté.

3 Transfer to a mixing bowl, cover,
and let chill for 1 hour.

4 Preheat the broiler. Place the
bread slices under the hot broiler
and toast for 2–3 minutes on each
side, until lightly browned.

5 Using a serrated knife, slice
off the crusts and cut through
the slices horizontally to make very
thin slices.

6 Preheat the oven to 300°F/150°C.
Stamp out circles using a 2-inch/
5-cm cookie cutter and place on a
baking sheet. Alternatively, cut each
piece of toast in half diagonally. Bake
the toasted circles in the preheated
oven for 15–20 minutes, until curled
and dry.

7 Spoon the pâté into individual
bowls. Serve each on a plate,
garnished with orange slices and fresh
dill sprigs, with the freshly baked toast.

broiled eggplant pâté

serves four

2 small eggplants

2 tbsp olive oil

juice of 1 lemon

4 tbsp sesame seed paste

2 garlic cloves, crushed (optional)

cucumber slices, to garnish

TO SERVE

carrot sticks and celery stalks

hot pita bread

1 Preheat the grill pan over high heat. Place the eggplants on the grill pan. Turning frequently, cook for about 10 minutes, or until the skins are black and blistered and the eggplants are very soft.

2 Remove the eggplants from the grill pan and let cool slightly. Cut in half and scoop out the insides into a mixing bowl. Mash with a fork to make a coarse paste.

3 Gradually add the olive oil, lemon juice, and sesame seed paste. Stir in the garlic, if using. Mix the pâté well, tasting and adjusting ingredient amounts, until you achieve the flavor and texture you like.

4 Transfer the mixture to an attractive bowl and garnish with cucumber. Serve with sticks of raw carrots and celery and hot pita bread.

cheese & bean pâté

serves eight

1 lb 12 oz/800 g canned cranberry
   or cannellini beans, rinsed
   and drained

1½ cups ricotta cheese

2 garlic cloves, coarsely chopped

4 tbsp lemon juice

4 oz/115 g butter, melted

3 tbsp chopped fresh
   flatleaf parsley

salt and pepper

corn oil, for oiling

TO GARNISH

fresh flatleaf parsley sprigs

lemon wedges

cheese-flavored focaccia fingers,
   to serve

1 Place the beans, cheese, garlic, lemon juice, and melted butter in a food processor and process to a smooth purée. Add the chopped parsley and salt and pepper to taste and process again briefly to mix.

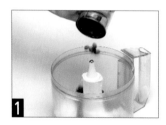

VARIATION

Instead of ricotta cheese, use strained cottage cheese for a slightly lighter alternative.

2 Lightly oil a plain ring mold. Scrape the mixture into the mold and smooth the surface. Cover with plastic wrap and let chill in the refrigerator until set.

3 To serve, turn out the pâté onto a serving dish and fill the center with parsley sprigs. Garnish with lemon wedges and serve with cheese-flavored focaccia fingers.

Pastries & Tarts

Every kind of pastry has its special appeal and appropriate accompaniments. Choose from crumbly basic pie dough with sumptuous  fillings, such as Asparagus & Cheese Tart (see page 68) and Broccoli Cashew Tart (see page 65); rich, flaky puff pastry with tender vegetables, such as Spinach & Potato Puff (see page 78) and Provençal Tart (see page 82); crisp, golden phyllo pastry encasing something spicy, such as Crab & Ginger Triangles (see page 97) and Vegetable Samosas (page 92); even light and airy Mini Choux Puffs with Shrimp Cocktail (see page 96). There are also delicious and dainty nibbles, such as Cheese Sablés (see page 101) or Deep-Fried Diamond Pastries (see page 102). All these morsels, packages, and slices are for popping in the mouth any time of day, either piping hot straight from the oven, invitingly warm or crisply cool.

onion tart

serves four

9 oz/250 g ready-made basic pie
   dough, thawed if frozen

all-purpose flour, for dusting

3 tbsp butter

2¾ oz/75 g bacon, chopped

1 lb 9 oz/700 g onions, thinly sliced

2 eggs, beaten

scant ½ cup freshly grated
   Parmesan cheese

1 tsp dried sage

salt and pepper

VARIATION

If you prefer, use red onions
instead of ordinary ones and
replace the dried sage with
thyme or oregano.

---

1 Roll out the dough on a lightly
floured counter and use to line a
9½-inch/24-cm loose-bottom tart pan.
Prick the base of the dough with a fork,
cover, and let chill in the refrigerator for
30 minutes.

2 Preheat the oven to 350°F/
180°C. Heat the butter in a pan,
add the bacon and onions, and cook
them over low heat for 25 minutes,
or until very soft. If they start to
brown, add 1 tablespoon of water to
the pan.

3 Add the beaten eggs, Parmesan,
and sage and season to taste
with salt and pepper. Spoon the
mixture into the prepared pastry shell.

4 Bake in the preheated oven for
20–30 minutes, or until the filling
has just set and the pastry is crisp and
golden. Let cool slightly in the pan,
then serve warm or cold.

garlic & pine nut tarts

serves four

4 slices whole-wheat bread

scant ⅓ cup pine nuts

5½ oz/150 g butter

5 garlic cloves, peeled and halved

2 tbsp chopped fresh oregano,
   plus extra to garnish

4 pitted black olives, halved

fresh oregano leaves, to garnish

1 Preheat the oven to 400°F/200°C. Using a rolling pin, flatten the bread slightly. With a cookie cutter, cut out 4 circles of bread to fit your individual tart pans—they should measure about 4 inches/10 cm across. Reserve the offcuts and let chill for 10 minutes, or until required.

2 Meanwhile, preheat the broiler. Place the pine nuts on a baking sheet and toast under the hot broiler for 2–3 minutes, or until golden. Make sure they do not burn.

3 Put the bread offcuts, pine nuts, butter, garlic, and oregano into a food processor and blend for 20 seconds. Alternatively, pound the ingredients by hand with a mortar and pestle. The mixture should have a coarse texture.

4 Spoon the pine nut and butter mixture into the lined pans and top with the olives. Bake in the preheated oven for 10–15 minutes, or until golden brown.

5 Transfer the tarts to serving plates and serve warm, garnished with oregano leaves.

instant pesto & goat cheese tartlets

makes twenty

7 oz/200 g ready-made puff pastry,
    thawed if frozen

all-purpose flour, for dusting

3 tbsp pesto

20 cherry tomatoes, each cut into
    3 slices

4 oz/115 g goat cheese

salt and pepper

fresh basil sprigs, to garnish

COOK'S TIP

These tartlets are even quicker to
make if you use the ready-rolled
variety of ready-made puff
pastry, which is available in
most large supermarkets.

1 Preheat the oven to 400°F/
200°C, then lightly flour a baking
sheet. Roll out the pastry on a floured
counter to ⅛ inch/3 mm thick. Cut out
20 circles with a 2-inch/5-cm plain
cutter and arrange the pastry circles on
the floured baking sheet.

2 Spread a little pesto on each
circle, leaving a margin around
the edge, then arrange 3 tomato slices
on top of each one.

3 Crumble the goat cheese over
and season to taste with salt and
pepper. Bake in the preheated oven for
10 minutes, or until the pastry is
puffed up, crisp, and golden. Garnish
with basil sprigs and serve warm.

mini cheese & onion tarts

serves twelve

BASIC PIE DOUGH

scant ¾ cup all-purpose flour, plus
    extra for dusting

¼ tsp salt

5½ tbsp butter, cut into small pieces

1–2 tbsp water

FILLING

1 egg, beaten

generous ⅓ cup light cream

1¾ oz/50 g Leicester
    cheese, grated

3 scallions, finely chopped

salt

cayenne pepper

COOK'S TIP

If you use 6 oz/175 g of
ready-made basic pie dough
instead of making it yourself,
these tarts can be made in a
matter of minutes.

1 To make the dough, sift the flour and salt into a large bowl. Add the butter and rub in with your fingertips until the mixture resembles bread crumbs. Stir in the water and mix to form a dough. Form the dough into a ball, cover with plastic wrap, and let chill in the refrigerator for 30 minutes.

2 Preheat the oven to 350°F/180°C. Roll out the dough on a lightly floured counter. Using a 3-inch/7.5-cm plain cutter, cut out 12 circles from the dough and use them to line a 12-hole tartlet pan.

3 To make the filling, whisk the beaten egg, cream, cheese, and scallions together in a pitcher. Season to taste with salt and cayenne pepper. Carefully pour the filling mixture into the pastry shells and bake in the preheated oven for 20–25 minutes, or until the filling is just set and the pastry is golden brown. Serve the tarts warm or cold.

greek feta & olive tartlets

makes twelve

butter, for greasing

all-purpose flour, for dusting

1 quantity Basic Pie Dough
(see page 62)

1 egg

3 egg yolks

1¼ cups heavy cream

salt and pepper

4 oz/115 g feta cheese (drained
weight)

6 pitted black olives, halved

12 small fresh rosemary sprigs

1 Preheat the oven to 400°F/
200°C. Grease 12 individual
2½-inch/6-cm tart pans, or the cups in
a 12-hole tartlet pan. On a floured
counter, roll out the dough to ⅛ inch/
3 mm thick. Using a plain cutter, cut
out 12 circles to line the prepared pans
and prick the bases with a fork. Press a
square of foil into each pastry shell and
bake in the preheated oven for
12 minutes. Remove the foil and bake
for an additional 3 minutes.

COOK'S TIP
Feta cheese is quite salty, so
there is no need to add much
extra salt when you season the
egg mixture in Step 2.

2 Place the egg, egg yolks, and
cream in a bowl, add salt and
pepper to taste, and beat together.

3 Crumble the feta cheese into the
pastry shells and spoon over the
egg mixture. Place half an olive and a
rosemary sprig on top of each tartlet,
then bake in the oven for 15 minutes,
or until the filling is just set. Serve
warm or cold.

broccoli cashew tart

serves six–eight

8 oz/225 g ready-made basic pie or
cheese dough, thawed if frozen

⅜ cup all-purpose flour, plus extra
for dusting

1 lb/450 g broccoli, cut into florets

salt and pepper

scant ½ cup unsalted cashews,
chopped

2 oz/55 g butter

¼ cup milk

3 oz/85 g cheese, such as Cheddar,
Emmental, Parmesan, or Gruyère,
coarsely grated

1 egg

pinch of cayenne pepper

1 Preheat the oven to 400°F/200°C.
Roll out the dough on a lightly
floured counter and use to line a
9-inch/23-cm shallow pie dish. Bake
blind, then remove from the oven
and let cool.

2 Steam the broccoli for 5 minutes,
then coarsely chop. Spread over
the pastry shell. Season to taste with
salt and pepper and sprinkle with nuts.

3 Melt the butter in a pan over
medium heat. Stir in the flour.
Gradually add the milk, stirring, until
the sauce has thickened. Season to
taste with salt and pepper. Add the
cheese and cook until melted.

4 Separate the egg. Stir
2 tablespoons of the cheese sauce
into the yolk, then add to the sauce
and mix. Remove from the heat. Whisk
the egg white until stiff. Fold into the
cheese sauce. Pour the sauce over the
broccoli and spread gently. Sprinkle with
cayenne pepper. Place the dish on a
baking sheet and bake in the oven for
20 minutes, then remove and let stand
for 5 minutes to rest before cutting.

goat cheese & oyster tartlets

makes twelve

generous ¾ cup all-purpose flour,
    plus extra for dusting

pinch of salt

3½ oz/100 g butter, chopped, plus
    extra for greasing

1 egg yolk

1 onion, chopped

12 oysters, cleaned

2 tbsp chopped fresh parsley

salt and pepper

7 oz/200 g goat cheese, crumbled

fresh flatleaf parsley sprigs,
    to garnish

1 Sift the flour and salt together in a bowl. Rub in 3¼ oz/90 g of the butter, then mix in the egg yolk to make a dough. Add a little cold water if needed. Shape into a ball and turn out onto a lightly floured counter. Roll out to a thickness of ¼ inch/5 mm. Grease 12 small tartlet pans, about 2¾ inches/7 cm in diameter, with butter. Line the pans with dough and trim the edges. Let the dough chill in the refrigerator for 45 minutes to prevent the pastry shrinking.

2 Preheat the oven to 400°F/200°C. Bake the tartlet shells for 10 minutes, until golden brown.

3 Meanwhile, heat the remaining butter over medium heat, add the onion, and cook for 4 minutes, stirring. Take the oysters out of their shells, add to the pan with the parsley, season, and cook for 1 minute. Remove the tartlets from the oven.

4 Divide 3½ oz/100 g of the goat cheese between them. Top with the oyster mixture, crumble over the remaining cheese, then bake for 10 minutes. Garnish with fresh parsley and serve hot.

asparagus & goat cheese tart

serves six

9 oz/250 g ready-made basic pie
    dough, thawed if frozen
all-purpose flour, for dusting
9 oz/250 g asparagus
1 tbsp vegetable oil
1 red onion, finely chopped
scant ¼ cup hazelnuts, chopped
7 oz/200 g goat cheese
2 eggs, beaten
4 tbsp light cream
salt and pepper

VARIATION

Omit the hazelnuts and sprinkle
grated Parmesan cheese over
the top of the tart just before
baking in the oven, if you prefer.

---

1 Roll out the dough on a lightly floured counter and use to line a 9½-inch/24-cm loose-bottom tart pan. Prick the base of the dough with a fork, cover, and let chill in the refrigerator for 30 minutes.

2 Preheat the oven to 375°F/190°C. Line the pastry shell with foil and dried beans and bake in the preheated oven for 15 minutes. Remove the foil and dried beans and cook for an additional 15 minutes.

3 Cook the asparagus in boiling water for 2–3 minutes, drain, and cut into bite-size pieces. Heat the oil in a small skillet and sauté the onion over low heat, stirring occasionally, until soft and lightly golden. Spoon the asparagus, onion, and hazelnuts into the pastry shell.

4 Beat the goat cheese, eggs, and light cream together until smooth. Alternatively, process in a food processor or blender until smooth. Season well with salt and pepper. Pour the mixture over the asparagus, onion, and hazelnuts. Bake in the preheated oven for 15–20 minutes, or until the filling is just set. Serve warm or cold.

masa tartlets with beans & avocado

serves four

8–10 tbsp masa harina

3 tbsp all-purpose flour

pinch of baking powder

about 1 cup warm water

vegetable oil, for cooking

8 oz/225 g canned pinto beans or
    refried beans, warmed

1 avocado, pitted, peeled, sliced,
    and tossed with lime juice

3 oz/85 g queso fresco, fresh cream
    cheese, or crumbled feta cheese

salsa of your choice

2 scallions, thinly sliced

TO GARNISH

fresh flatleaf parsley sprigs

lemon wedges

1 Mix the masa harina with the flour and baking powder in a bowl, then mix in enough warm water to make a firm yet moist dough.

2 Pinch off about a walnut-size piece of dough and, using your fingers, shape into a tiny tartlet shape, pressing and pinching to make it as thin as possible without falling apart. Repeat with the remaining dough.

3 Heat a layer of oil in a deep skillet until it is smoking. Add a batch of tartlets to the hot oil and cook, spooning the hot fat into the center of the tartlets and turning once, until golden on all sides.

4 Using a slotted spoon, remove the tartlets from the hot oil and drain on paper towels. Place on a baking sheet and keep warm in the oven on a low temperature while cooking the remaining tartlets.

5 Fill each tartlet shell with the warmed beans, avocado, cheese, salsa, and scallions. Garnish with parsley and lemon wedges and serve.

brazil nut & mushroom pie

serves four

1¾ cups whole-wheat flour, plus
extra for dusting
3½ oz/100 g butter or margarine,
diced
4 tbsp water
milk, to glaze
FILLING
1 tbsp butter or margarine
1 onion, chopped
1 garlic clove, finely chopped
4½ oz/125 g white
mushrooms, sliced
1 tbsp all-purpose flour
⅔ cup vegetable stock
1 tbsp tomato paste
1⅛ cups Brazil nuts, chopped
1⅜ cups fresh whole-wheat
bread crumbs
2 tbsp chopped fresh parsley
½ tsp pepper

1 To make the dough, sift the flour into a mixing bowl and add any bran remaining in the strainer. Add the butter and rub in with your fingertips until the mixture resembles fine bread crumbs. Stir in the water and bring together to form a dough. Wrap in foil and let chill in the refrigerator for 30 minutes.

2 Preheat the oven to 400°F/200°C. To make the filling, melt the butter in a skillet over low heat. Add the onion, garlic, and mushrooms and cook for 5 minutes, or until softened. Add the flour and cook for 1 minute, stirring constantly. Gradually add the stock, stirring, until the sauce is smooth and starting to thicken. Stir in the tomato paste, nuts, bread crumbs, parsley, and pepper. Remove the skillet from the heat and let cool slightly.

3 Roll out two-thirds of the dough on a lightly floured counter and use it to line an 8-inch/20-cm loose-bottom tart pan. Spread the filling in the pastry shell. Brush the edges of the pastry with milk. Roll out the remaining dough to fit the top of the pie. Press the edges to seal, make a slit in the top of the dough to allow steam to escape during cooking and brush with milk.

4 Bake in the preheated oven for 30–40 minutes, or until golden brown. Serve warm.

potato & spinach triangles

serves four

2 tbsp butter, melted, plus extra
   for greasing

8 oz/225 g waxy potatoes,
   finely diced

1 lb 2 oz/500 g fresh baby spinach

2 tbsp water

1 tomato, seeded and chopped

¼ tsp chili powder

½ tsp lemon juice

salt and pepper

8 oz/225 g (8 sheets) phyllo pastry,
   thawed if frozen

crisp salad, to serve

LEMON MAYONNAISE

⅔ cup mayonnaise

2 tsp lemon juice

rind of 1 lemon

1 Preheat the oven to 375°F/
   190°C. Lightly grease a baking
sheet with a little butter.

2 Cook the potatoes in a pan of
   lightly salted boiling water for
10 minutes, or until tender. Drain
thoroughly and place in a mixing bowl.

3 Meanwhile, put the spinach into
   a large pan with the water, cover,
and cook, stirring occasionally, over
low heat for 2 minutes, or until
wilted. Drain the spinach thoroughly,
squeezing out the excess moisture,
and add to the potatoes.

4 Stir in the tomato, chili powder,
   and lemon juice. Season to taste
with salt and pepper.

5 Lightly brush the sheets of phyllo
   pastry with melted butter. Spread
out 4 of the sheets and lay a second
sheet on top of each. Cut them into
rectangles about 8 x 4 inches/
20 x 10 cm.

6 Spoon a portion of the potato and
   spinach mixture onto one end of
each rectangle. Fold a corner of the
pastry over the filling, fold the pointed
end back over the pastry strip, then
fold over the remaining pastry to form
a triangle.

7 Place the triangles on the
   prepared baking sheet and bake
in the preheated oven for 20 minutes,
or until golden brown.

8 To make the mayonnaise, mix the
   mayonnaise, lemon juice, and
lemon rind together in a small bowl.
Serve the Potato & Spinach Triangles
either warm or cold with the lemon
mayonnaise and a crisp salad.

phyllo tartlets with avocado salsa

makes twenty

TARTLET SHELLS

2 sheets phyllo pastry (about
    8 x 12 inches/20 x 30 cm),
    thawed if frozen
3 tbsp melted butter, plus extra
    for greasing

AVOCADO SALSA

1 large avocado
1 small red onion, finely chopped
1 fresh chili, seeded and
    finely chopped
2 tomatoes, peeled, seeded, and
    finely chopped
juice of 1 lime
2 tbsp chopped fresh cilantro
salt and pepper

COOK'S TIP

The pastry shells can be made up
to a week in advance and stored
in an airtight container. Make
the salsa just before serving.
Once the shells are filled, serve
them at once, otherwise they
will go soft.

1 Preheat the oven to 350°F/ 180°C. To make the tartlet shells, working with 1 sheet of phyllo pastry at a time and keeping the rest covered with a cloth, brush the pastry sheet with melted butter. With a sharp knife, cut the sheet into 2-inch/5-cm squares.

2 Grease 20 cups in mini muffin trays and line each one with 3 greased phyllo pastry squares, setting each one at an angle to the others. Repeat until all the pastry is used up. Bake in the preheated oven for 6–8 minutes, or until crisp and golden. Transfer to a wire rack to cool.

3 To make the Salsa, peel the avocado and remove the pit. Cut the flesh into small dice and place in a bowl with the onion, chili, tomatoes, lime juice, cilantro, and salt and pepper to taste. Gently mix, then divide the salsa between the pastry shells and serve at once.

spinach, feta & tomato triangles

serves four

2 tbsp olive oil

2 tbsp finely chopped shallot

2½ cups fresh spinach, rinsed
  and shredded

salt and pepper

2 sheets phyllo pastry

4 oz/115 g feta cheese (drained
  weight), crumbled

6 sun-dried tomatoes,
  finely chopped

4 oz/115 g butter, melted, plus extra
  for greasing

1 Preheat the oven to 400°F/
200°C. Heat the oil in a pan over
medium heat and cook the shallot for
2–3 minutes. Add the spinach,
increase the heat to high, and cook,
stirring constantly, for 2–3 minutes.
Remove from the heat and drain.
Coarsely chop, season to taste with
salt and pepper, and let cool.

2 Cut each sheet of phyllo pastry
into 6 strips. Place a spoonful of
spinach in a corner of each pastry strip.
Sprinkle cheese and tomatoes on top.
Fold the pastry over at right angles to
make a triangle, enclosing the filling.
Continue folding in this way all the
way down the strip to make a
triangular package.

3 Brush the edges of each triangle
with melted butter, then transfer
to a greased baking sheet. Brush the
tops of the packages with more butter.
Bake in the preheated oven for
10 minutes, or until the pastry is
golden and crisp. Remove from the
oven and serve at once.

anchovy, olive & cheese triangles

makes forty

2 oz/55 g canned anchovies
  in olive oil, drained and
  coarsely chopped

⅓ cup black olives, pitted and
  coarsely chopped

4 oz/115 g Manchego or Cheddar
  cheese, finely grated

¾ cup all-purpose flour, plus extra
  for dusting

4 oz/115 g unsalted butter, diced

½ tsp cayenne pepper, plus extra
  for dusting

1 Place the anchovies, olives, cheese, flour, butter, and cayenne pepper in a food processor and pulse until a dough forms. Turn out and shape into a ball. Wrap in foil and let chill in the refrigerator for 30 minutes.

2 Preheat the oven to 400°F/ 200°C. Unwrap the dough, knead on a lightly floured counter, and roll out thinly. Using a sharp knife, cut it into strips about 2 inches/5 cm wide. Cut diagonally across each strip, turning the knife in alternate directions, to make triangles.

3 Arrange the triangles on 2 baking sheets and dust lightly with cayenne pepper. Bake in the preheated oven for 10 minutes, or until golden brown. Transfer to wire racks to cool completely.

little feta & spinach crescents

makes 16

1 lb/450 g fresh spinach, coarse
   stalks removed

4 scallions, finely chopped

2 eggs, lightly beaten

1 tbsp chopped fresh parsley

1 tbsp chopped fresh dill

12 oz/350 g feta cheese
   (drained weight)

pepper

8 sheets phyllo pastry (about
   4½ x 7 inches/12 x 18 cm),
   thawed if frozen

olive oil, for brushing

1 Preheat the oven to 375°F/190°C. Pour water to a depth of about ½ inch/1 cm into a large pan and bring to a boil. Add the spinach and cook, turning once, for 1–2 minutes, or until just wilted. Drain well, then squeeze out as much excess liquid as you can with your hands. Finely chop the spinach and place in a large bowl. Add the scallions, eggs, parsley, and dill. Crumble in the feta and season to taste with pepper. Mix together thoroughly.

2 Keep the phyllo pastry sheets covered with plastic wrap to prevent them drying out. Take a sheet of phyllo, brush with oil, and cut in half lengthwise. Spread a little of the filling across one corner, leaving a small margin on either side. Roll up securely but not too tightly and curl in the ends to make a crescent shape. Place on a baking sheet. Repeat with remaining phyllo pastry sheets and filling.

3 Brush the crescents with oil and bake in the preheated oven for 25 minutes, or until golden and crisp. Remove from the oven and let stand on the baking sheet for 5 minutes, then transfer to a wire rack to cool. Serve at room temperature.

spinach & potato puff

serves four

12 oz/350 g ready-made puff
　　pastry, thawed if frozen

all-purpose flour, for dusting

1 lb/450 g fresh spinach or chard,
　　washed thoroughly

salt and pepper

½ tsp finely grated nutmeg

12 oz/350 g small new potatoes,
　　cooked, peeled, and cut into
　　thick slices

8 oz/225 g mozzarella cheese,
　　sliced or grated

1 egg

1 tbsp water

butter, for greasing

1 Preheat the oven to 375°F/
190°C. Cut the pastry into
2 pieces, 1 twice as large as the other.
Roll the pastry out on a floured counter
and trim into 2 rectangles. Keep the
trimmings and let the pastry rest for
10 minutes.

2 Cook the spinach or chard in a
pan over medium heat for
3–4 minutes. Drain, chop, and add salt
and pepper to taste and the nutmeg.
Arrange a layer of potatoes on the
larger rectangle, leaving a margin of
pastry on all sides. Season to taste
with salt and pepper. Spread the
spinach over the potatoes. Top with
cheese and a final layer of potatoes.

3 Beat the egg in a bowl and stir in
the water. Fold the margins of the
pastry to the center. Brush with the
beaten egg. Put the smaller rectangle
on top and seal.

4 Transfer to a greased baking
sheet and brush with beaten egg.
Roll out the trimmings and cut into
shapes. Place on top of the pastry
package and brush with beaten egg.
Bake in the preheated oven for
30 minutes. Remove from the oven
and let the package rest for 5 minutes
before slicing and serving.

lattice tart

butter, for greasing

2 quantities Rich Basic Pie Dough
　　(see page 86), chilled

all-purpose flour, for dusting

lightly beaten egg, to glaze

FILLING

1 lb/450 g frozen spinach, thawed

2 tbsp olive oil

1 large onion, chopped

2 garlic cloves, finely chopped

2 eggs, lightly beaten

1 cup ricotta cheese

½ cup freshly grated
　　Parmesan cheese

freshly grated nutmeg

salt and pepper

1 Preheat the oven to 400°F/
200°C. Lightly grease a
9-inch/23-cm loose-bottom tart pan
with butter. To make the filling, drain
the spinach and squeeze out as much
moisture as possible. Heat the oil in a
large, heavy-bottom skillet. Add the
onion and cook, stirring occasionally,
for 5 minutes, or until softened. Add
the garlic and spinach and cook,
stirring occasionally, for 10 minutes.
Remove the skillet from the heat, let
cool slightly, then beat in the eggs,
the ricotta, and Parmesan cheese.
Season to taste with nutmeg, salt,
and pepper.

2 Roll out two-thirds of the dough
on a lightly floured counter and
use it to line the prepared tart pan,
leaving it overhanging the sides.
Spoon in the spinach mixture,
spreading it evenly over the base.

3 Roll out the remaining dough on
a lightly floured counter and cut
into ¼-inch/5-mm strips. Arrange the
strips in a lattice pattern on top of the
tart, pressing the ends down securely
to seal. Trim any excess dough. Brush
with the beaten egg and bake in the
preheated oven for 45 minutes, or until
golden brown. Transfer to a wire rack
to cool slightly before removing
from the pan.

COOK'S TIP

When preparing dough for a tart
pan, roll out away from you in
one direction only. Rotate the
dough in between strokes to
ensure an even thickness.

VARIATION

Egg glaze gives the dough
a shiny finish. If you prefer a
matt finish to your dough,
brush with milk rather
than beaten egg.

provençal tart

serves six

9 oz/250 g ready-made puff pastry,
    thawed if frozen

all-purpose flour, for dusting

3 tbsp olive oil

2 red bell peppers, diced

2 green bell peppers, diced

⅔ cup heavy cream

1 egg

salt and pepper

2 zucchini, sliced

COOK'S TIP

This recipe could be used to
make 6 individual tarts—use
6 x 4-inch/15 x 10-cm pans and
bake them in the oven for
20 minutes, or until just set and
golden brown.

---

1 Roll out the pastry on a lightly floured counter and use to line an 8-inch/20-cm loose-bottom tart pan. Cover and let chill in the refrigerator for 20 minutes.

2 Preheat the oven to 350°F/180°C. Heat 2 tablespoons of the oil in a skillet and sauté the bell peppers over low heat, stirring frequently, for 8 minutes, or until softened. Whisk the cream and egg together in a bowl and season to taste with salt and pepper. Stir in the cooked bell peppers.

3 Heat the remaining oil in a separate skillet and sauté the zucchini slices over medium heat, stirring frequently, for 4–5 minutes, or until lightly browned. Pour the egg and bell pepper mixture into the pastry shell. Arrange the zucchini slices around the edge of the tart.

4 Bake in the preheated oven for 35–40 minutes, or until just set and golden brown. Serve at once or let cool in the pan.

lentil & red bell pepper tart

serves six

PIE DOUGH

1¾ cups whole-wheat flour

3½ oz/100 g butter or margarine,
   cut into small pieces

4 tbsp water

FILLING

scant 1 cup split red lentils, rinsed

1¼ cups vegetable stock

1 tbsp butter or margarine

1 onion, chopped

2 red bell peppers, seeded
   and diced

1 tsp yeast extract

1 tbsp tomato paste

3 tbsp chopped fresh parsley

pepper

VARIATION

Add corn kernels to the tart in
Step 4 for a colorful and tasty
change, if you prefer.

1 To make the dough, sift the flour into a mixing bowl and add any bran remaining in the strainer. Add the butter and rub in with your fingertips until the mixture resembles fine bread crumbs. Stir in the water and bring together to form a dough. Wrap in foil and let chill in the refrigerator for 30 minutes.

2 Preheat the oven to 400°F/200°C. To make the filling, put the lentils into a pan with the stock and bring to a boil. Reduce the heat and let simmer for 10 minutes, or until the lentils are tender and can be mashed to a purée.

3 Melt the butter in a small pan, add the onion and bell peppers and cook until just soft.

4 Add the lentil purée, yeast extract, tomato paste, and parsley. Season to taste with pepper. Mix until thoroughly combined.

5 On a lightly floured counter, roll out the dough and use to line a 9½-inch/24-cm loose-bottom tart pan. Prick the base of the dough with a fork and spoon the lentil mixture into the pastry shell.

6 Bake in the preheated oven for 30 minutes, or until the filling is firm to the touch.

mushroom & onion quiche

serves four

butter, for greasing

1 quantity Rich Basic Pie Dough
  (see page 86), chilled

all-purpose flour, for dusting

FILLING

2 oz/55 g unsalted butter

3 red onions, halved and sliced

12 oz/350 g mixed exotic
  mushrooms, such as cèpes,
  chanterelles, and morels

2 tsp chopped fresh thyme

1 egg

2 egg yolks

generous ⅓ cup heavy cream

salt and pepper

COOK'S TIP

If you are in a hurry, you can
use ready-prepared basic pie
dough, but if it is frozen, make
sure that you thaw it thoroughly
before use.

1 Preheat the oven to 375°F/
190°C. Lightly grease a
9-inch/23-cm loose-bottom tart pan
with butter. Roll out the dough on a
lightly floured counter and use to line
the pan. Prick the base, cover, and let
chill in the refrigerator for 30 minutes.
Line with foil, fill with dried beans, and
bake in the preheated oven for
25 minutes. Remove the foil and beans
and let cool on a wire rack. Reduce the
oven temperature to 350°F/180°C.

2 To make the filling, melt the
butter in a large, heavy-bottom
skillet. Add the onions, cover, and
cook over very low heat, stirring
occasionally, for 20 minutes. Add the
mushrooms and thyme and cook for an
additional 10 minutes. Spoon the
mixture into the pastry shell and place
the pan on a baking sheet.

3 Lightly beat the egg with the egg
yolks and cream and season to
taste with salt and pepper. Pour the
mixture over the mushroom filling and
bake in the oven for 20 minutes, or
until the filling is set and golden. Serve
hot or at room temperature.

quiche lorraine

makes 1 x 9-inch/ 23-cm quiche

RICH BASIC PIE DOUGH

generous 1 cup all-purpose flour, plus extra for dusting

pinch of salt

4 oz/115 g butter, diced

1 oz/25 g romano cheese, grated

4–6 tbsp ice water

FILLING

4 oz/115 g Gruyère cheese, thinly sliced

2 oz/55 g Roquefort cheese, crumbled

6 oz/175 g rindless lean bacon, broiled until crisp

3 eggs

⅔ cup heavy cream

salt and pepper

1 To make the dough, sift the flour with the salt into a bowl. Add the butter and rub in with your fingertips until the mixture resembles bread crumbs. Stir in the romano cheese, then stir in enough of the water to bind. Shape the dough into a ball, wrap in foil, and let chill in the refrigerator for 15 minutes.

2 Preheat the oven to 375°F/ 190°C. Unwrap and roll out the dough on a lightly floured counter. Use to line a 9-inch/23-cm tart pan. Place the pan on a baking sheet. Prick the base of the pastry shell all over with a fork, line with foil or waxed paper, and fill with dried beans. Bake in the preheated oven for 15 minutes, or until the edges are set and dry. Remove the beans and lining and bake the pastry shell for an additional 5–7 minutes, or until golden. Let cool slightly.

3 For the filling, arrange the cheese over the base of the pastry shell, then crumble the bacon evenly on top. In a bowl, beat the eggs with the cream until thoroughly combined. Add salt and pepper to taste. Pour the mixture into the pastry shell and return to the oven for 20 minutes, or until the filling is golden and set.

4 Remove from the oven and let cool in the pan for 10 minutes. Transfer to a wire rack to cool completely. Cover and store in the refrigerator, but return to room temperature before serving.

pissaladière

serves four

4 tbsp olive oil, plus extra for oiling

1 lb 9 oz/700 g red onions,
   thinly sliced

2 garlic cloves, crushed

2 tsp superfine sugar

2 tbsp red wine vinegar

salt and pepper

1–2 tbsp flour, for dusting

12 oz/350 g fresh ready-made
   puff pastry

TOPPING

3½ oz/100 g canned anchovies

12 green olives, pitted

1 tsp dried marjoram

1 Lightly oil a jelly-roll pan. Put the remaining oil in a large pan and heat gently. Add the onions and garlic and cook over low heat for 30 minutes, stirring occasionally.

2 Add the sugar and vinegar to the pan and season well with salt and pepper.

3 Preheat the oven to 425°F/ 220°C. On a lightly floured counter, roll out the pastry to a rectangle measuring 13 x 9 inches/ 33 x 23 cm. Place the pastry rectangle in the prepared pan, using your fingers to push the pastry into the corners.

4 Remove the onion mixture from the heat and spread over the pastry shell.

5 Arrange the anchovies and olives on top, then sprinkle with the dried marjoram.

6 Bake in the preheated oven for 20–25 minutes, or until the pissaladière is lightly golden. Serve the pissaladière piping hot, straight from the oven.

COOK'S TIP

Cut the pissaladière into squares or triangles and serve at an outdoor party.

pancake rolls

serves four

4 tsp vegetable oil

1–2 garlic cloves, crushed

1 cup fresh ground pork

8 oz/225 g bok choy, shredded

4½ tsp light soy sauce

½ tsp sesame oil

8 egg roll skins, 10 inches/25 cm
    square, thawed if frozen

oil, for deep-frying

CHILI SAUCE

generous ¼ cup superfine sugar

¼ cup rice vinegar

2 tbsp water

2 fresh red chilies, finely chopped

1 Heat the oil in a preheated wok. Add the garlic and stir-fry for 30 seconds. Add the ground pork and stir-fry for 2–3 minutes, or until lightly colored.

2 Add the bok choy, soy sauce, and sesame oil to the wok and stir-fry for 2–3 minutes. Remove from the heat and set aside to cool.

3 Spread out the egg roll skins on a counter and spoon 2 tablespoons of the pork mixture along one edge of each. Roll the skin over once and fold in the sides. Roll up completely to make a sausage shape, brushing the edges with a little water to seal. Set the pancake rolls aside for 10 minutes to seal firmly.

4 To make the chili sauce, heat the sugar, vinegar, and water in a small pan, stirring until the sugar dissolves. Bring the mixture to a boil and boil rapidly until a light syrup forms. Remove from the heat and stir in the chilies. Let the sauce cool before serving.

5 Heat the oil for deep-frying in a wok until almost smoking. Reduce the heat slightly and deep-fry the pancake rolls, in batches if necessary, for 3–4 minutes, or until golden brown. Remove from the oil with a slotted spoon and drain on paper towels. Serve on warmed serving plates with the chili sauce.

böreks

makes twenty

8 oz/225 g feta cheese
  (drained weight)

2 tbsp chopped fresh mint

2 tbsp chopped fresh parsley

1½ tbsp chopped fresh dill

pinch of freshly grated nutmeg

pepper

20 sheets phyllo pastry (about
  4½ x 7 inches/12 x 18 cm),
  thawed if frozen

olive oil, for brushing

1 Preheat the oven to 375°F/190°C. Crumble the feta into a bowl and add the mint, parsley, dill, and nutmeg. Season to taste with pepper and mix thoroughly.

2 Keep the phyllo pastry sheets covered with plastic wrap to prevent them drying out. Take a sheet of phyllo and brush with oil. Place a second sheet on top and brush with oil. Cut in half lengthwise. Place a teaspoonful of the cheese mixture at one end of a pastry strip. Fold the pastry over at right angles to make a triangle, enclosing the filling. Continue folding in this way all the way down the strip to make a triangular package.

3 Repeat with the remaining phyllo pastry sheets and filling. Brush the tops of the pastries with a little more oil and bake in the preheated oven for 15–20 minutes, or until golden and crisp. Remove from the oven and transfer to a wire rack to cool. Serve at room temperature.

The Böreks can also be deep-fried.

1

2

2

vegetable samosas

makes thirty

3 large potatoes, cut into chunks

salt

¾ cup frozen peas

generous ⅓ cup frozen corn
    kernels, thawed

2 shallots, finely chopped

1 tsp ground cumin

1 tsp ground coriander

2 fresh green chilies, seeded and
    finely chopped

2 tbsp chopped fresh mint

2 tbsp chopped fresh cilantro

4 tbsp lemon juice

15 sheets phyllo pastry (about
    4½ x 7 inches/12 x 18 cm),
    thawed if frozen

melted butter, for brushing

peanut or corn oil, for deep-frying

mango chutney, to serve

1 Place the potatoes in a pan and add cold water to cover and a pinch of salt. Bring to a boil, then reduce the heat, cover, and let simmer for 15–20 minutes, or until tender. Meanwhile, cook the peas according to the instructions on the package, then drain. Drain the potatoes, return to the saucepan, and mash coarsely with a potato masher or fork. Add the peas to the potatoes, then transfer to a bowl.

2 Add the corn, shallots, cumin, ground coriander, chilies, mint, fresh cilantro, and lemon juice and season to taste with salt. Mix well.

3 Keep the phyllo pastry sheets covered with plastic wrap to prevent them drying out. Take a sheet of phyllo, brush with melted butter, and cut in half lengthwise. Place a tablespoonful of the filling in a corner of the pastry strip. Fold the pastry over at right angles to make a triangle, enclosing the filling. Continue folding in this way all the way down the strip to make a triangular package. Repeat with the remaining phyllo and filling.

4 Heat the oil in a deep-fat fryer or large pan to 350–375°F/ 180–190°C, or until a cube of bread browns in 30 seconds. Add the samosas, in batches, and cook until golden brown. Remove with a slotted spoon and drain on paper towels. Alternatively, bake the samosas in a preheated oven at 400°F/200°C, for 10–15 minutes, or until golden brown. Serve the samosas hot or at room temperature with mango chutney.

sausage rolls

makes forty-eight

1 lb/450 g sausagemeat

1 tsp Worcestershire sauce

beaten egg, to glaze

PIE DOUGH

1½ cups all-purpose flour, plus

    extra for dusting

pinch of salt

½ tsp mustard powder

4 oz/115 g butter, diced

2–3 tbsp iced water

1 For the dough, sift the flour into a bowl with the salt and mustard powder. Add the butter and rub in with your fingertips until the mixture resembles bread crumbs. Gradually stir in enough of the water to make a soft, but not sticky, dough. Shape the dough into a ball, wrap in foil, and let chill in the refrigerator for 20 minutes.

2 Mix the sausagemeat and Worcestershire sauce together in a bowl until thoroughly combined and the meat is broken up. Divide the mixture into 12 portions and roll each one between the palms of your hands to make a 6-inch/15-cm long sausage.

3 Preheat the oven to 375°F/ 190°C. Roll out the dough on a lightly floured counter to a rectangle measuring 8 x 18 inches/20 x 46 cm. Using a sharp knife, cut the dough into 12 rectangles, each measuring about 2 x 6 inches/5 x 15 cm. Place a sausagemeat roll on a dough rectangle and brush the long edges of the dough with water. Roll the dough over the sausagemeat to enclose it, then cut the roll into 4 equal pieces. Repeat with the remaining dough and sausagemeat rolls.

4 Arrange the sausage rolls on 2 baking sheets, seam-side down. Brush with the beaten egg and bake in the preheated oven for 10 minutes, or until golden brown and cooked through. Remove from the oven and transfer the sausage rolls to a wire rack to cool.

mini choux puffs with shrimp cocktail

makes twenty-two

CHOUX PASTRY

2 oz/55 g butter, plus extra
　for greasing

⅔ cup water

scant ½ cup all-purpose flour, sifted

2 eggs, beaten

FILLING

2 tbsp mayonnaise

1 tsp tomato paste

5 oz/140 g small cooked, shelled
　peeled shrimp

1 tsp Worcestershire sauce

salt

Tabasco sauce

1 Boston lettuce, shredded

cayenne pepper, to garnish

COOK'S TIP

The choux puffs can be filled up
to 3 hours in advance, then left
in the refrigerator until you are
ready to serve them. Bring
them to room temperature
before serving.

1 Preheat the oven to 350°F/
180°C. Grease a baking sheet. To
make the choux pastry, place the butter
and water in a large, heavy-bottom
pan and bring to a boil. Add the flour,
all at once, and beat thoroughly until
the mixture leaves the sides of the pan.
Let cool slightly, then vigorously beat in
the eggs, 1 at a time. Place 22 walnut-
size spoonfuls of the mixture onto the
baking sheet, spaced ¾ inch/2 cm
apart. Bake in the preheated oven for
35 minutes, or until light, crisp and
golden. Transfer to a wire rack to cool.
Cut a ¼-inch/5-mm slice from the top
of each puff.

2 To make the filling, place the
mayonnaise, tomato paste,
shrimp, and Worcestershire sauce in a
bowl. Add salt and Tabasco sauce to
taste, and mix together until combined.

3 Place a few lettuce shreds in the
bottom of each puff, making
some protrude at the top. Spoon the
shrimp mixture on top and dust with a
little cayenne pepper before serving.

crab & ginger triangles

makes twelve

3 oz/85 g butter, melted, plus extra
  for greasing

7 oz/200 g fresh or canned
  crabmeat, drained

6 scallions, finely chopped, plus
  extra to garnish

1-inch/2.5-cm piece fresh
  gingerroot, peeled and grated

2 tsp soy sauce

pepper

12 sheets phyllo pastry, thawed
  if frozen

1 Preheat the oven to 350°F/
  180°C. Grease a baking sheet.
Place the crabmeat, scallions, ginger,
and soy sauce in a bowl. Add pepper
to taste, mix together and set aside.
Working with 1 sheet of phyllo pastry
at a time and keeping the remainder
covered with plastic wrap to prevent
them drying out, brush a pastry sheet
with melted butter, fold in half
lengthwise and brush again
with butter.

2 Place a spoonful of the crab
  mixture in a corner of the pastry
strip. Fold the pastry over at right
angles to make a triangle, enclosing
the filling. Continue folding in this way
all the way down the strip to make a
triangular package.

3 Place the package on the
  prepared baking sheet. Repeat
with the remaining pastry and crab
mixture. Brush each package with
melted butter. Bake in the preheated
oven for 20–25 minutes, or until crisp
and golden brown. Garnish with extra
chopped scallions and serve warm.

COOK'S TIP

It is a good idea to use fresh
crabmeat for this recipe, if it is
available, instead of less-
flavorsome canned crabmeat.

seafood phyllo packages

makes twenty-four

3½ oz/100 g canned red
   salmon, drained
3½ oz/100 g canned
   crabmeat, drained
2 tbsp chopped fresh parsley
8 scallions, finely chopped
8 sheets phyllo pastry
   (about 8 x 12 inches/
   20 x 30 cm), thawed if frozen
melted butter, for brushing
corn oil, for oiling

1 Remove and discard the skin and
bones from the salmon, place in a
bowl, and flake the flesh with a fork.
Remove and discard any cartilage from
the crabmeat, place in another bowl,
and flake gently with a fork. Divide the
parsley and scallions between the
bowls and mix well.

2 Preheat the oven to 400°F/
200°C. Keep the phyllo pastry
sheets covered with plastic wrap to
prevent them drying out. Take a sheet
of pastry, brush with melted butter,
then place a second sheet on top. Cut
into 4-inch/10-cm squares. Place a
teaspoonful of the salmon mixture on
each square. Brush the edges of the
pastry with melted butter, then draw
together to make little pouches. Press
to seal. Repeat with 2 more sheets of
phyllo and the salmon mixture, then
repeat with the remaining sheets of
phyllo and the crabmeat mixture.

3 Lightly oil a baking sheet and
place the packages on it. Bake in
the preheated oven for 15 minutes, or
until golden. Serve warm.

thyme crescents

serves eight

3½ oz/100 g butter, softened, plus
   extra for greasing
9 oz/250 g ready-made puff pastry,
   thawed if frozen
1 garlic clove, crushed
1 tsp lemon juice
1 tsp dried thyme
salt and pepper

COOK'S TIP

Dried herbs have a stronger flavor than fresh ones, which makes them perfect for these pastries. The crescents can be made with other dried herbs of your choice, such as rosemary and sage, or mixed herbs.

1 Preheat the oven to 400°F/200°C. Lightly grease a baking sheet.

2 On a lightly floured counter, roll out the pastry to form a 10-inch/25-cm circle and cut into 8 wedges.

3 In a small bowl, mix the butter, garlic, lemon juice, and thyme together until soft. Season to taste with salt and pepper.

4 Spread a little of the butter and thyme mixture on to each wedge of pastry, dividing it equally between the wedges.

5 Carefully roll up each wedge, starting from the wide end.

6 Arrange the crescents on the prepared baking sheet, cover, and chill in the refrigerator for 30 minutes.

7 Dampen the baking sheet with cold water. This will create a steamy atmosphere in the oven while the crescents are baking and help the pastries to rise.

8 Bake in the preheated oven for 10–15 minutes, or until the crescents are well risen and golden brown.

cheese sablés

makes thirty-five

5½ oz/150 g butter, diced, plus
  extra for greasing
1 cup all-purpose flour, plus extra
  for dusting
5½ oz/150 g sharp cheese, grated
1 egg yolk
sesame seeds, for sprinkling

1 Preheat the oven to 400°F/
200°C. Lightly grease several
baking sheets with a little butter.

2 Mix the flour and cheese together
in a bowl.

3 Add the butter to the cheese and
flour mixture and rub in with your
fingertips until the mixture resembles
bread crumbs.

4 Stir in the egg yolk and mix to
form a dough. Wrap in plastic
wrap. Let chill for 30 minutes.

5 Roll out the dough thinly on a
lightly floured counter. Cut out
circles with a 2½-inch/6-cm cutter,
rerolling the trimmings to make
35 cookies.

6 Place the circles onto the
prepared baking sheets and
sprinkle the sesame seeds over the top.

7 Bake in the preheated oven for
20 minutes, or until lightly
golden brown.

8 Carefully transfer the cookies to
a wire rack and let cool slightly
before serving.

VARIATION

For a sweet variation of these
traditional French cookies,
substitute the grated rind of
1 lemon for the cheese and stir in
scant ⅔ cup superfine sugar at
the end of Step 2. Beat the egg
yolk with 1 tablespoon of brandy
or rum before adding it to the
mixture. Roll out the dough, cut
out circles and bake as above.

COOK'S TIP

Cut out any shape you like for
your savory cookies. Children will
enjoy them cut into animal
shapes or other fun designs.

deep-fried diamond pastries

1 cup all-purpose flour

1 tsp baking powder

½ tsp salt

1 tbsp black cumin seeds

generous ⅓ cup water

1¼ cups oil

dal, to serve (optional)

COOK'S TIP

Black cumin seeds are used here for their strong aromatic flavor. White cumin seeds may not be used as a substitute.

1 Place the flour in a large mixing bowl.

2 Add the baking powder, salt, and the black cumin seeds and stir to mix well.

3 Add the water to the dry ingredients and mix to form a soft, elastic dough.

4 Roll out the dough on a clean counter until about ¼ inch/ 5 mm thick.

5 Using a sharp knife, score the dough to form diamond shapes. Reroll the dough trimmings and cut out more diamond shapes until all of the dough has been used up.

6 Heat the oil in a deep-fat fryer or large pan to 350–375°F/ 180–190°C, or until a cube of bread browns in 30 seconds.

7 Carefully place the pastry diamonds in the oil, in batches if necessary, and deep-fry until golden brown.

8 Remove the diamond pastries with a slotted spoon and let drain on paper towels. Serve with a dal for dipping or store in an airtight container and serve when required.

Meat & Poultry Nibbles

Here is a whole range of party-food favorites for meat-lovers to grapple with, some rather more "hands-on" than others–chicken wings,

for instance, which come in Sticky Ginger or San Francisco-style (see pages 111 and 116), or drumsticks with a tasty honey & mustard coating (see page 108). For something yet more digitally challenging, choose between spareribs Chinese-style (see page 130) or with honey and chili (see page 124), depending on your tastes and mood. Easier to handle and universally appealing are kabobs—both in miniature form, with tasty nuggets of chicken and beef interspersed with vegetables threaded onto toothpicks, or standard-size, including spicy satay. Other speared treats to savor are Pigs in Blankets (see page 126) and Crispy Bacon Nibbles (see page 122)—perfect fare to make a social occasion go with a swing.

oven-fried chicken wings

serves four

12 chicken wings

1 egg

½ cup milk

4 heaping tbsp all-purpose flour

1 tsp paprika

salt and pepper

2 cups bread crumbs

2 oz/55 g butter

VARIATION

For a hotter result, replace the paprika with chili powder.

1 Preheat the oven to 425°F/ 220°C. Separate the chicken wings into 3 pieces each. Discard the bony tip. Beat the egg with the milk in a shallow dish. Combine the flour, paprika, and salt and pepper to taste in a separate shallow dish. Place the bread crumbs in another shallow dish.

2 Dip the chicken pieces into the egg to coat well, then drain and roll in the seasoned flour. Remove, shaking off any excess, and roll the chicken in the bread crumbs, gently pressing them onto the surface, then shaking off any excess.

3 Melt the butter in the preheated oven in a shallow roasting pan large enough to hold all the chicken pieces in a single layer. Arrange the chicken, skin side down, in the pan and bake in the oven for 10 minutes. Turn and bake for an additional 10 minutes, or until the chicken is tender and the juices run clear when a skewer is inserted into the thickest part of the meat.

4 Remove the chicken from the pan and arrange on a large platter. Serve hot or at room temperature.

honey & mustard drumsticks

makes twelve

12 chicken drumsticks

¾ cup honey

6 tbsp whole-grain mustard

2 tbsp Dijon mustard

2 tbsp white wine vinegar

3 tbsp corn oil

fresh parsley sprigs, to garnish

1 Using a sharp knife, make several slashes in each chicken drumstick, then place them in a large, nonmetallic dish.

2 Mix together the honey, both types of mustard, vinegar, and oil in a pitcher, whisking well to combine. Pour the marinade over the chicken, turning and stirring to coat. Cover with plastic wrap and place the chicken in the refrigerator to marinate for at least 2–3 hours, or preferably overnight.

3 Preheat the broiler to medium. Place the drumsticks on a broiler rack and cook under the hot broiler, turning and brushing frequently with the marinade, for 25 minutes, or until the chicken is tender and the juices run clear when a skewer is inserted into the thickest part of the meat. Set aside to cool, then arrange on a serving platter and garnish with parsley sprigs.

miniature beef kabobs

serves four

4 oz/115 g sirloin or rump steak

4 white mushrooms, cut into
　½-inch/1-cm cubes

½ small onion, cut into
　½-inch/1-cm cubes

SPICY TOMATO MARINADE

¼ cup tomato juice

¼ cup beef stock

1 tbsp Worcestershire sauce

1 tbsp lemon juice

2 tbsp dry sherry

few drops of Tabasco sauce

2 tbsp vegetable oil

1 tbsp minced celery

1 Cut the steak into ½-inch/1-cm cubes. Combine all the marinade ingredients in a large, nonmetallic bowl, whisk well and stir in the meat, mushrooms, and onion. Cover with plastic wrap and let marinate in the refrigerator for 30 minutes.

2 Drain off the marinade and set aside. Place alternating pieces of steak and vegetables on toothpicks, taking care not to pack them together too tightly.

3 Preheat a griddle pan or heavy-bottom skillet over high heat. Place the kabobs in the pan and cook, turning frequently, for 5 minutes, or until gently browned and cooked through. Baste occasionally with the reserved marinade.

4 Pile the kabobs high on platters and serve at once.

miniature chicken kabobs

serves four

1 skinless, boneless chicken breast,
    cut into ½-inch/1-cm pieces
½ small onion, cut into ½-inch/
    1-cm pieces
½ red bell pepper, seeded and cut
    into ½-inch/1-cm pieces
½ green bell pepper, seeded and cut
    into ½-inch/1-cm pieces
SWEET & SOUR MARINADE
½ cup orange, grapefruit,
    or pineapple juice
1 tbsp sweet sherry
¼ cup dark soy sauce
¼ cup chicken stock
2 tbsp cider vinegar
1 tsp tomato paste
2 tbsp brown sugar
pinch of ground ginger

3 Prepare the vegetables. Place alternating pieces of chicken and vegetables on toothpicks, taking care not to pack them together too tightly. Reserve the marinade.

1 To make the marinade, combine all the liquid ingredients in a nonmetallic bowl. Add the tomato paste, sugar, and ginger. Mix well, then add the chicken and vegetables and stir to coat thoroughly.

2 Cover and let marinate in the refrigerator for 30 minutes.

4 Preheat a grill pan or heavy-bottom skillet over high heat. Place the kabobs in the pan and cook, turning frequently, for 10 minutes, or until browned and cooked through. Baste for the first 5 minutes only with the reserved marinade.

5 Pile the kabobs high on platters and serve at once.

sticky ginger chicken wings

serves four

2 garlic cloves, coarsely chopped

1 piece preserved ginger in syrup,
coarsely chopped

1 tsp coriander seeds

2 tbsp preserved ginger syrup

2 tbsp dark soy sauce

1 tbsp lime juice

1 tsp sesame oil

12 chicken wings

TO GARNISH

lime wedges

fresh cilantro leaves

1 Place the garlic, ginger, and coriander seeds in a mortar and crush to a paste with a pestle, gradually working in the ginger syrup, soy sauce, lime juice, and oil.

VARIATION

If you can't get chicken wings for this recipe, use drumsticks instead, but make sure that they are thoroughly cooked before serving.

2 Tuck the pointed tip of each chicken wing underneath the thicker end of the wing to make a neat triangular shape. Place in a large, nonmetallic bowl.

3 Add the garlic and ginger paste to the bowl and toss the chicken wings in the mixture to coat evenly. Cover and marinate in the refrigerator for several hours, or overnight.

4 Preheat the broiler to medium. Cook the chicken wings in a single layer on a foil-lined broiler pan under the hot broiler for 12–15 minutes, turning occasionally, or until golden brown, tender, and the juices run clear when a skewer is inserted into the thickest part of the meat.

5 Alternatively, preheat the barbecue and cook on a lightly oiled grill over medium–hot coals. Transfer to serving plates, garnish with lime wedges and cilantro and serve.

chicken balls with dipping sauce

serves four–six

2 large skinless, boneless
   chicken breasts

3 tbsp vegetable oil

2 shallots, finely chopped

½ celery stalk, finely chopped

1 garlic clove, crushed

2 tbsp light soy sauce

1 small egg, lightly beaten

salt and pepper

1 bunch scallions

scallion tassels, to garnish

DIPPING SAUCE

3 tbsp dark soy sauce

1 tbsp rice wine or dry sherry

1 tsp sesame seeds

1 Cut the chicken into ¾-inch/
2-cm pieces. Heat half the oil in
a large skillet. Add the chicken and
stir-fry over high heat for 2–3 minutes,
or until golden. Remove the chicken
with a slotted spoon and set aside.

2 Add the shallots, celery, and
garlic to the skillet and stir-fry for
1–2 minutes, or until the vegetables
are softened but not browned.

3 Place the chicken, shallots, celery,
and garlic in a food processor and
process until finely minced. Add half
the light soy sauce, just enough egg to
make a fairly firm mixture, and salt and
pepper to taste.

4 Trim the scallions and cut into
2-inch/5-cm lengths. Set aside
until required. Make the dipping sauce
by mixing the dark soy sauce, rice wine
or sherry, and sesame seeds together
in a bowl. Set aside.

5 Form the chicken mixture into
16–18 walnut-size balls between
the palms of your hands. Heat the
remaining oil in the skillet and stir-fry
the balls, in small batches, for
4–5 minutes, or until golden brown.
As each batch is cooked, drain on
paper towels and keep hot.

6 Stir-fry the reserved scallions for
1–2 minutes, until they start to
soften, then stir in the remaining light
soy sauce. Serve with the chicken balls
and dipping sauce, garnished with
scallion tassels.

honeyed chicken wings

serves four

1 lb/450 g chicken wings

2 tbsp peanut oil

2 tbsp light soy sauce

2 tbsp hoisin sauce

2 tbsp honey

2 garlic cloves, crushed

1 tsp sesame seeds

MARINADE

1 dried red chili

½–1 tsp chili powder

½–1 tsp ground ginger

finely grated rind of 1 lime

COOK'S TIP

Make the dish in advance and
freeze the chicken wings.
Thaw completely, cover with
foil and heat thoroughly in
a medium–hot oven.

1 To make the marinade, crush the chili in a mortar with a pestle. Mix together the crushed chili, chili powder, ginger, and lime rind in a small bowl.

2 Thoroughly rub the spice mixture into the chicken wings with your fingertips. Cover and place in the refrigerator for at least 2 hours to allow the flavors to penetrate the chicken.

3 Heat the oil in a large preheated wok or skillet.

4 Add the chicken wings and cook, turning frequently, for 10–12 minutes, or until golden and crisp. Drain off any excess oil.

5 Add the soy sauce, hoisin sauce, honey, garlic, and sesame seeds to the wok, turning the chicken wings to coat them all over.

6 Reduce the heat and cook, turning the chicken wings frequently, for 20–25 minutes, or until tender and the juices run clear when a skewer is inserted into the thickest part of the meat. Serve hot.

san francisco wings

makes twelve

5 tbsp dark soy sauce

2 tbsp dry sherry

1 tbsp rice vinegar

2-inch/5-cm strip of orange rind,
   pith removed

juice of 1 orange

1 tbsp brown sugar

1 star anise

1 tsp cornstarch, mixed to a paste
   with 3 tbsp water

1 tbsp finely chopped fresh
   gingerroot

1 tsp chili sauce

3 lb 5 oz/1.5 kg chicken wings

1 Preheat the oven to 400°F/
200°C. Place the soy sauce,
sherry, vinegar, orange rind, orange
juice, sugar, and star anise in a pan
and mix well. Bring to a boil over
medium heat, then stir in the
cornstarch paste. Continue to boil,
stirring constantly, for 1 minute, or until
thickened. Remove the pan from the
heat and stir in the chopped ginger
and chili sauce.

2 Remove and discard the tips from
the chicken wings and place the
wings in a single layer in an ovenproof
dish or roasting pan. Pour the sauce
over the wings, turning and stirring
to coat.

3 Bake in the preheated oven for
35–40 minutes, turning and
basting with the sauce occasionally,
until the chicken is tender and
browned and the juices run clear when
a skewer is inserted into the thickest
part of the meat. Serve hot or warm.

sticky chicken drummers

serves four

8 skinless chicken drumsticks

3 tbsp mango chutney

2 tsp Dijon mustard

2 tsp corn oil

1 tsp paprika

1 tsp black mustard seeds,
    coarsely crushed

½ tsp ground turmeric

2 garlic cloves, chopped

salt and pepper

SALSA

1 mango, diced

1 tomato, finely chopped

½ red onion, thinly sliced

2 tbsp chopped fresh cilantro

salt and pepper

VARIATION

Use mild curry powder instead
of the turmeric.

1 Preheat the oven to 400°F/200°C. Using a small, sharp knife, slash each drumstick 3–4 times, then place in a roasting pan.

2 Mix the mango chutney, mustard, oil, spices, garlic, and salt and pepper to taste together in a small bowl. Spoon over the chicken drumsticks, turning until they are coated all over with the glaze.

3 Bake in the preheated oven for 40 minutes, brushing with the glaze several times during cooking (but not for the last few minutes), until the chicken drumsticks are well browned and tender and the juices run clear when a skewer is inserted into the thickest part of the meat.

4 To make the salsa, mix all the ingredients together in a small bowl. Season to taste with salt and pepper, cover, and let chill in the refrigerator until required.

5 Arrange the chicken drumsticks on a serving plate and serve hot or cold with the mango salsa.

117

chicken or beef satay

serves six

4 boneless, skinless chicken
    breasts or 1 lb 10 oz/750 g
    rump steak, trimmed

lime wedges, to serve

MARINADE

1 small onion, finely chopped

1 garlic clove, crushed

1-inch/2.5-cm piece fresh
    gingerroot, grated

2 tbsp dark soy sauce

2 tsp chili powder

1 tsp ground coriander

2 tsp brown sugar

1 tbsp lemon or lime juice

1 tbsp vegetable oil

SAUCE

1¼ cups coconut milk

4 tbsp crunchy peanut butter

1 tbsp Thai fish sauce

1 tsp lemon or lime juice

salt and pepper

1 Using a sharp knife, trim any fat from the chicken or beef and discard. Cut the meat into thin strips, about 3 inches/7.5 cm long.

2 To make the marinade, put all the ingredients into a shallow, nonmetallic dish and mix well. Add the meat and coat well in the marinade. Cover with plastic wrap and let marinate in the refrigerator for at least 2 hours, or preferably overnight.

3 Remove the meat from the marinade and thread the pieces, concertina-style, onto presoaked bamboo or thin wooden skewers.

4 Preheat the broiler to medium. Put the satays under the hot broiler and cook for 8–10 minutes, turning and brushing occasionally with the marinade for the first 4–5 minutes only, until cooked through.

5 To make the sauce, mix the ingredients together in a pan. Bring to a boil and cook for 3 minutes. Season to taste with salt and pepper.

6 Pour the sauce into a bowl and serve with the satays and lime wedges for squeezing over.

118

beef kabobs

serves four

8 scallions

1 lb 9 oz/700 g rump steak,
    cut into cubes

8 cherry tomatoes, halved

1 tbsp whole-grain mustard

1 tsp Worcestershire sauce

½ tsp balsamic vinegar

4 tbsp corn oil

salt and pepper

1 Preheat the broiler to medium. Cut the scallions into 4–5-inch/10–13-cm lengths and halve lengthwise. Thread the steak cubes, scallion lengths, and cherry tomato halves alternately onto 4 metal or presoaked wooden skewers. Arrange them on a broiler rack.

COOK'S TIP

It is much quicker to use metal skewers for this dish because wooden ones need to be soaked in warm water for 30 minutes before using to prevent them burning under the broiler or on the barbecue.

2 Mix the mustard, Worcestershire sauce, and vinegar together in a small bowl. Whisk in the oil and season to taste with salt and pepper.

3 Brush the kabobs with the flavored oil and cook under the hot broiler for 4 minutes. Turn over, brush with the flavored oil again and cook for 4 minutes. Transfer to a large serving plate and serve at once.

pork satay

serves four

1 lb 2 oz/500 g pork fillet

SAUCE

scant 1 cup unsalted peanuts

2 tsp hot chili sauce

¾ cup coconut milk

2 tbsp soy sauce

1 tbsp ground coriander

pinch of ground turmeric

1 tbsp brown sugar

salt

TO GARNISH

fresh flatleaf parsley or cilantro

cucumber leaves (see Cook's Tip)

fresh red chilies

COOK'S TIP

To make cucumber leaves, slice a thick chunk from the side of a cucumber, and cut to shape. Cut grooves in the cucumber flesh in the shape of leaf veins.

1 To make the sauce, preheat the broiler to medium. Sprinkle the peanuts on a baking sheet and toast under the hot broiler until golden brown, turning once or twice. Let cool, then grind in a food processor. Alternatively, chop the peanuts finely.

2 Put the ground peanuts into a small pan with the hot chili sauce, coconut milk, soy sauce, ground coriander, turmeric, sugar, and salt. Heat gently, stirring constantly and taking care not to burn the sauce on the bottom of the pan. Reduce the heat to very low and cook gently for 5 minutes.

3 Meanwhile, trim any fat from the pork. Cut the pork into cubes and thread onto 8 presoaked bamboo skewers. Place the kabobs on a rack covered with foil in a broiler pan.

4 Put half the peanut sauce into a small serving bowl. Brush the skewered pork with the remaining sauce and place under the hot broiler for 10 minutes, turning and basting frequently for the first 5 minutes only, until thoroughly cooked through.

5 Serve the pork with the reserved peanut sauce and garnish with parsley or cilantro leaves, cucumber leaves, and chilies.

crispy bacon nibbles

serves four

12 lean bacon slices

12 dates, prunes, scallops, or water
chestnuts

1 Holding each bacon slice down
firmly with a knife or fork on a
cutting board, use the back of a knife
to smooth and stretch its length.

2 Place a date, prune, scallop, or
water chestnut at one end of
each slice and roll up. Secure with
a toothpick to keep it closed.

3 Preheat a ridged griddle pan
or broiler until very hot. Place
the bacon rolls in the pan or on the
broiler rack and cook, turning once,
for 5–10 minutes, or until the bacon
is crisp and well browned. Whatever
is wrapped in the bacon must be
thoroughly cooked or heated through.
Alternatively, you could cook the
bacon rolls on a flat baking sheet for
25–30 minutes in an oven preheated
to 400°F/200°C.

4 Transfer to a large platter and
serve at once.

VARIATION

Strips of prosciutto, brushed with
a herb-flavored oil, could be
used in place of the bacon.

three-flavor pinwheels

makes fifty–sixty

HAM & CREAM CHEESE
PINWHEELS

¾ cup cream cheese

4 large slices lean ham

4 tbsp snipped fresh chives

BEEF & HORSERADISH
PINWHEELS

½ cup heavy cream

2 tbsp creamed horseradish

4 large slices medium-rare
    roast beef

SALMON & DILL CREAM
PINWHEELS

1 cup heavy cream

2 tbsp chopped fresh dill

pepper

4 large or 8 medium slices
    smoked salmon

4 tbsp lemon juice

1 For the Ham & Cream Cheese
Pinwheels, spread the cream
cheese evenly over the slices of ham.
Sprinkle with the chives. Roll up each
slice tightly and wrap individually in
plastic wrap. Let chill in the refrigerator
for 1 hour.

2 For the Beef & Horseradish
Pinwheels, whip the cream in a
bowl until stiff, then fold in the
creamed horseradish. Spread the
mixture evenly over the slices of beef.
Roll up each slice tightly and wrap
individually in plastic wrap. Let chill in
the refrigerator for 1 hour.

3 For the Smoked Salmon & Dill
Cream Pinwheels, whip the cream
in a bowl until stiff, then fold in the dill
and pepper to taste. Spread the
mixture evenly over the slices of
smoked salmon. Roll up each slice
tightly and wrap individually in plastic
wrap. Let chill in the refrigerator for
1 hour.

4 When ready to serve, unwrap
the rolls one at a time and slice
into bite-size pieces. Before slicing
the Smoked Salmon & Dill Cream
Pinwheels, sprinkle with a little
lemon juice. Spear each pinwheel
on a toothpick and arrange on a
serving platter.

roasted spareribs with honey & chili

makes thirty

2 tbsp peanut or corn oil

1 onion, chopped

1 garlic clove, finely chopped

1 fresh green chili, seeded and
finely chopped

3 tbsp honey

2 tbsp tomato paste

1 tbsp white wine vinegar

pinch of chili powder

⅔ cup chicken stock

1 lb 12 oz/800 g pork spareribs

1 Preheat the oven to 375°F/
190°C. Heat the oil in a heavy-
bottom pan over medium heat. Add
the onion, garlic, and chili and cook,
stirring occasionally, for 5 minutes,
or until softened. Stir in the honey,
tomato paste, vinegar, chili powder,
and stock and bring to a boil. Reduce
the heat and let simmer, stirring
occasionally, for 15 minutes, or until
the sauce has thickened.

2 Meanwhile, chop the spareribs
into 2-inch/5-cm lengths and
place in a roasting pan. Pour the sauce
over them, turning and stirring to coat.
Roast in the preheated oven for 1 hour,
turning and basting with the sauce
frequently, until the ribs are thoroughly
browned and sticky.

3 Remove the ribs from the oven,
transfer to a warmed serving
dish, and serve at once.

thai-spiced sausages

serves four

1¾ cups fresh lean ground pork

¾ cup cooked rice

1 garlic clove, crushed

1 tsp Thai red curry paste

1 tsp pepper

1 tsp ground coriander

½ tsp salt

3 tbsp lime juice

2 tbsp chopped fresh cilantro

3 tbsp peanut oil

soy sauce, to serve

TO GARNISH

cucumber slices

fresh red chili strips

COOK'S TIP

These sausages can also be served as an appetizer—shape the mixture slightly smaller to make 16 bite-size sausages. Serve with a soy dipping sauce.

1 Place the pork, rice, garlic, curry paste, pepper, ground coriander, salt, lime juice, and fresh cilantro in a bowl and knead together with your hands to mix evenly.

2 Use your hands to form the mixture into 12 small sausage shapes. If you can buy sausage casings, fill the casings and twist at intervals to separate the sausages.

3 Heat the oil in a large skillet over medium heat. Add the sausages, in batches if necessary, and cook, turning them over occasionally, for 8–10 minutes, or until they are evenly golden brown and cooked through. Transfer to a serving plate, garnish with cucumber slices, and a few strips of chili and serve hot with soy sauce.

pigs in blankets

makes forty-eight

16 large, good quality sausages

4 tbsp Dijon mustard

48 no-soak prunes

16 rindless smoked bacon slices

VARIATION

Try using no-soak dried apricots in place of the prunes and another mustard of your choice, such as whole-grain. Choose a mixture of different-flavored sausages for variety, such as herb or spicy.

1 Cut a deep slit along the length of each sausage without cutting all the way through. Spread the mustard evenly over the cut sides of the slits. Place 3 prunes inside each slit, pressing the sausages firmly together.

2 Gently stretch each bacon slice with the back of a knife. Wind a slice around each sausage to hold it together.

3 Preheat the broiler to medium, then cook under the hot broiler, turning frequently, for 15 minutes, or until cooked through. Transfer to a cutting board and cut each "pig" into 3 pieces, each containing a prune. Spear with toothpicks, arrange on a plate, and serve.

chorizo & olive frittata

serves four

2 oz/55 g butter

1 small onion, finely chopped

1 small green or red bell pepper,
  seeded and finely chopped

2 tomatoes, seeded and diced

2 small cooked potatoes, diced

4½ oz/125 g chorizo sausage or
  salami, finely chopped

8 green or black olives, pitted and
  finely chopped

8 large eggs

2 tbsp milk

salt and pepper

2 oz/55 g Cheddar cheese, grated

TO GARNISH

mixed salad greens

pimiento strips

1 Melt the butter in a large skillet over medium heat. Add the onion, bell pepper, and tomatoes, stir well, then cook for 3–4 minutes, or until softened. Mix in the potatoes, chorizo or salami, and olives. Cook gently for 5 minutes to heat through. In a small bowl, beat the eggs with the milk and salt and pepper to taste.

2 Pour over the vegetables in the skillet and reduce the heat to low. Cook the eggs, occasionally lifting the edges and tilting the skillet to let the liquid run to the outside.

3 Preheat the broiler to high. When the eggs are mostly set, with only a little liquid egg in the middle, sprinkle over the cheese. Place the skillet under the hot broiler and cook for 2 minutes, or until the cheese has melted and is golden brown. Remove the skillet from the broiler and let the frittata cool before cutting into wedges. Garnish with mixed salad greens and pimiento strips and serve.

chorizo & artichoke heart quesadillas

serves four–six

1 chorizo sausage

1 large mild fresh green chili or
　 green bell pepper (optional)

8–10 marinated artichoke hearts or
　 canned artichoke hearts, drained
　 and diced

4 soft corn tortillas, warmed

2 garlic cloves, finely chopped

12 oz/350 g cheese, grated

1 tomato, diced

2 scallions, thinly sliced

1 tbsp chopped fresh cilantro

1 Preheat the broiler to medium. Dice the chorizo. Heat a heavy-bottom skillet, add the chorizo, and cook until it browns in places.

2 If using the chili or green bell pepper, place under the hot broiler and cook for 10 minutes, or until the skin is charred and the flesh softened. Place in a plastic bag, twist to seal well, and let stand for 20 minutes. Carefully remove the skin from the chili or bell pepper with a knife, then seed and chop the flesh.

3 Arrange the browned chorizo and artichoke hearts on the corn tortillas, then transfer half to a baking sheet.

4 Sprinkle with the chopped garlic, then the grated cheese. Place under the hot broiler and cook until the cheese melts and sizzles. Repeat with the remaining tortillas.

5 Sprinkle the warmed tortillas with the tomato, scallions, chili, or bell pepper, if using, and the cilantro. Cut into wedges. Serve at once.

spareribs chinese-style

serves four

2 lb 4 oz/1 kg Chinese-style

  spareribs

½ lemon

½ small orange

1-inch/2.5-cm piece fresh

  gingerroot

2 garlic cloves

1 small onion, chopped

2 tbsp soy sauce

2 tbsp rice wine or dry sherry

½ tsp Thai seven-spice powder

2 tbsp honey

1 tbsp sesame oil

lemon twists, to garnish

orange wedges, to serve

COOK'S TIP

If you don't have a food
processor, grate the rind and
squeeze the juice from the citrus
fruits. Grate the ginger, crush the
garlic, and finely chop the onion.
Mix these ingredients together
with the remaining ingredients.

1 Preheat the oven to 350°F/
180°C. Place the spareribs in a
wide roasting pan, cover loosely with
foil, and cook in the preheated oven
for 30 minutes.

2 Meanwhile, remove any pips
from the lemon and orange and
place them in a food processor with
the ginger, garlic, onion, soy sauce, rice
wine or sherry, seven-spice powder,
honey, and oil. Process until smooth.

3 Increase the oven temperature to
400°F/200°C. Pour off any fat
from the spareribs, then spoon the
puréed mixture over the spareribs and
toss to coat evenly.

4 Return the ribs to the oven and
roast for 40 minutes, turning and
basting them occasionally, until
golden brown. Garnish the ribs with
lemon twists and serve hot with
orange wedges.

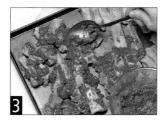

Fish Nibbles

Fish dishes usually have a certain elegance and sophistication, especially when daintily packaged and presented. Here we have the tried and tested canapé classics, such as Deviled Eggs (see page 134), Traditional English Potted Shrimp (see page 136), and Devils & Angels on Horseback (see page 155), together with some exotic seafood specialties, such as Caribbean Crab Cakes (see page 145) and Jumbo Shrimp Rolls with Sweet Chili Sauce (see page 138). Additional delectable fish morsels are especially designed to be delicately dipped in an accompanying sauce, such as Parsley Fish Balls (see page 144) and Fish Cakes with Sweet & Sour Sauce (see page 150). Presentation makes some of the dishes simply irresistible to the eye and taste buds alike, such as Crispy Crab Won Tons (see page 146) and Mussels in Spiced Batter (see page 147), perfectly cradled in their shells.

deviled eggs

8 hard-cooked eggs

2 tbsp canned, drained, and
    flaked tuna

4 canned anchovies in olive oil,
    drained, 1 tsp oil reserved, and
    coarsely chopped

6 black olives, pitted

1 tsp capers

COOK'S TIP

You can use the oil from the
tuna, if canned in olive oil,
instead of the anchovy oil, or add
some extra virgin olive oil or a
herb-flavored oil.

1 Shell the eggs and cut in half lengthwise. Scoop the yolks out into a bowl, or place in a food processor, with the tuna, 2 anchovies, 4 olives, and all the capers.

2 Blend the ingredients together to make a smooth paste, adding the reserved anchovy oil to achieve the correct consistency.

3 Arrange the egg whites on a serving platter. Fill the hollows with the yolk mixture using either a teaspoon or a pastry bag fitted with a star tip. Make sure that the filling is piled high.

4 Cut the remaining anchovies and olives into tiny strips. Sprinkle over the filled eggs to garnish and serve at once.

traditional english potted shrimp

serves eight

10 oz/280 g unsalted butter

3 pieces blade mace

pinch of freshly grated nutmeg

pinch of cayenne pepper

1 lb/450 g cooked shelled shrimp

TO GARNISH

fresh parsley sprigs

lemon slices

slices brown bread, spread with
  unsalted butter, to serve

1 Place 6 oz/175 g of the butter in a
small, heavy-bottom pan and add
the mace, nutmeg, and cayenne
pepper. Melt over the lowest possible
heat, stirring occasionally.

2 Add the shrimp and cook, stirring
constantly, for 2 minutes, or until
heated through. Do not allow the
mixture to boil.

3 Remove the pan from the heat,
then remove and discard the
mace. Spoon the mixture into a serving
dish and level the surface. Cover and
set aside to cool, then let chill in the
refrigerator until set. (Traditionally,
potted shrimp are served in ramekins
as individual appetizers. If you want to
do this, divide the mixture equally
between 8 small ramekins.)

4 When the potted shrimp have set,
place the remaining butter in a
small, heavy-bottom pan. Melt over
low heat, then skim off the scum that
has formed on the surface. Carefully
pour off the clear liquid into a bowl,
leaving the white milk solids in the
bottom of the pan. Spoon the clarified
butter over the top of the potted
shrimp to make a thin, covering layer.
Cover and return to the refrigerator
until set.

5 Garnish the potted shrimp with
parsley sprigs and lemon slices
and serve with the buttered slices of
brown bread.

jumbo shrimp rolls with sweet chili sauce

makes sixteen

SWEET CHILI SAUCE

1 small fresh red Thai
　chili, seeded

1 tsp honey

4 tbsp soy sauce

SHRIMP ROLLS

2 tbsp fresh cilantro leaves

1 garlic clove

1½ tsp Thai red curry paste

16 won ton skins

1 egg white, lightly beaten

16 raw jumbo shrimp, shelled and
　tails left intact

corn oil, for deep-frying

1 To make the dip, finely chop the chili and place in a small bowl. Add the honey and soy sauce and stir well. Set aside until required.

2 To make the shrimp rolls, finely chop the cilantro and garlic and place in a bowl. Add the curry paste and mix well.

3 Brush each won ton skin with egg white and place a small dab of the cilantro mixture in the center. Place a shrimp on top.

4 Fold the won ton skin over, enclosing the shrimp and leaving the tail exposed. Repeat with the other jumbo shrimp.

5 Heat the oil in a deep-fat fryer or large pan to 350–375°F/ 180–190°C, or until a cube of bread browns in 30 seconds. Deep-fry the shrimp, in small batches, for 1–2 minutes each, or until golden brown and crisp. Drain on paper towels. Serve with the dip.

VARIATION

If you prefer, replace the won ton skins with phyllo pastry—use a long strip of pastry, place the paste and a shrimp on one end, then brush with egg white. Wrap the pastry around the shrimp to enclose and deep-fry.

mini shrimp egg rolls

makes about thirty

1¾ oz/50 g dried rice vermicelli

1 carrot, cut into short thin sticks

1¾ oz/50 g snow peas, thinly
    shredded lengthwise

3 scallions, finely chopped

3½ oz/100 g cooked shelled shrimp

2 garlic cloves, crushed

1 tsp sesame oil

2 tbsp light soy sauce

1 tsp chili sauce

7 oz/200 g phyllo pastry, cut into
    6-inch/15-cm squares

1 egg white, beaten

2½ cups vegetable oil, for
    deep-frying

dark soy sauce, sweet chili sauce, or
    Sweet & Sour Dipping Sauce (see
    page 150), for dipping

1 Cook the rice vermicelli according to the instructions on the package. Drain well. Coarsely chop and set aside. Bring a pan of lightly salted water to a boil over medium heat. Add the carrot and snow peas and blanch for 1 minute. Drain and refresh under cold running water. Drain again and pat dry on paper towels. Mix with the noodles and add the scallions, shrimp, garlic, sesame oil, soy sauce, and chili sauce. Set aside.

2 Fold the phyllo pastry squares in half diagonally to form triangles. Lay a triangle on the counter, with the fold facing you, and place a spoonful of the mixture in the center. Roll over the wrapper to enclose the filling, then bring over the corners to enclose the ends of the roll. Brush the point of the egg roll farthest from you with beaten egg white and continue rolling to seal. Make about 30 egg rolls.

3 Fill a deep-fat fryer or large pan about one-third full with vegetable oil and heat to 350–375°F/ 180–190°C, or until a cube of bread browns in 30 seconds. Add the egg rolls, in batches of 4–5, and deep-fry for 1–2 minutes, or until golden and crisp. Drain on paper towels. Keep warm while you cook the remaining egg rolls.

4 Serve with soy sauce, sweet chili sauce or Sweet & Sour Dipping Sauce for dipping.

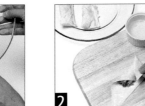

shrimp & chicken sesame toasts

makes seventy-two

4 skinless, boneless chicken thighs

3½ oz/100 g cooked,

   shelled shrimp

1 small egg, beaten

3 scallions, finely chopped

2 garlic cloves, crushed

2 tbsp chopped fresh cilantro

1 tbsp Thai fish sauce

salt and pepper

12 slices white bread,

   crusts removed

generous ⅓ cup sesame seeds

corn oil, for pan-frying

shredded scallion curls,

   to garnish

1 Place the chicken and shrimp in a food processor and process until very finely chopped. Add the egg, scallions, garlic, cilantro, fish sauce, and salt and pepper to taste, and pulse for a few seconds to mix well. Transfer to a large bowl.

2 Spread the mixture evenly over the slices of bread, right to the edges. Sprinkle the sesame seeds over a plate and press the chicken-and-shrimp-topped side of each slice of bread into them to coat evenly.

3 Using a sharp knife, cut the bread into small rectangles, making 6 per slice.

COOK'S TIP

If you're catering for a party, it's a good idea to make the toasts in advance, then store them in the refrigerator or freezer. Cover and let chill for up to 3 days, or place in a sealed container or plastic bag and freeze for up to 1 month. Thaw overnight in the refrigerator, then pop into a hot oven for 5 minutes to reheat.

4 Heat a ½-inch/1-cm depth of oil in a wide skillet until very hot. Pan-fry the bread rectangles quickly, in batches, for 2–3 minutes, or until golden brown all over, turning them over once.

5 Drain the toasts well on paper towels, transfer to a serving dish, and garnish with shredded scallion curls. Serve hot.

shrimp on crisp tortilla wedges

serves eight–ten

1 lb 2 oz/500 g cooked,
    shelled shrimp

4 garlic cloves, finely chopped

½ tsp mild chili powder

½ tsp ground cumin

juice of 1 lime

1 ripe tomato, diced

salt

6 soft corn tortillas

vegetable oil, for cooking

2 avocados

scant 1 cup sour cream

mild chili powder, to garnish

lime wedges, to serve

1 Place the shrimp in a nonmetallic bowl with the chopped garlic, chili powder, cumin, lime juice, and diced tomato. Add salt to taste and stir gently to mix. Cover and let chill in the refrigerator for at least 4 hours or overnight to allow all the flavors to mingle.

2 Cut the tortillas into wedges. Heat a little oil in a nonstick skillet, add a batch of tortilla wedges, and cook over medium heat until crisp. Repeat with the remaining wedges and transfer to a serving platter.

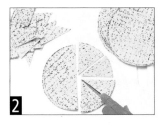

3 Cut each avocado in half around the pit. Twist apart, then remove the pit with a knife. Carefully peel off the skin and dice the flesh. Gently stir the avocado into the shrimp mixture.

4 Top each tortilla wedge with a small mound of the shrimp and avocado mixture. Finish with a little sour cream and garnish with a light sprinkling of mild chili powder. Serve at once while hot and crisp with lime wedges.

COOK'S TIP

For speed, you can use crisp corn tortillas (tostadas) or nacho chips (not too salty) instead of the soft corn tortillas.

VARIATION

Substitute diced mozzarella or mild fresh romano cheese for the shrimp and let marinate for a few hours.

parsley fish balls

serves four

1 lb/450 g white fish fillets, skinned

1 onion, quartered

2 eggs

4 tbsp matzo meal or bread crumbs

1 tbsp finely chopped fresh parsley

salt and pepper

oil, for deep-frying

Sweet & Sour Dipping Sauce
   (see page 150), to serve

1 Cut the fish into large chunks. Place in a food processor with the onion. Blend to make a coarse paste, then transfer to a large mixing bowl.

2 Add the eggs and matzo meal or bread crumbs. Stir to bind. Add the parsley and salt and pepper to taste.

3 Heat the oil in a wok or large pan to 350–375°F/180–190°C, or until a cube of bread browns in 30 seconds.

4 Shape the fish mixture into small balls or patties and gently drop into the oil. Cook until golden brown. Carefully remove from the oil and drain on a plate lined with paper towels.

5 Serve the fish balls hot or at room temperature, accompanied by the Sweet & Sour Dipping Sauce.

caribbean crab cakes

makes sixteen

1 potato, cut into chunks

4 scallions, chopped

1 garlic clove, chopped

1 tbsp chopped fresh thyme

1 tbsp chopped fresh basil

1 tbsp chopped fresh cilantro

8 oz/225 g white crabmeat, drained
if canned and thawed if frozen

½ tsp Dijon mustard

½ fresh green chili, seeded and
finely chopped

1 egg, lightly beaten

salt and pepper

all-purpose flour, for dusting

corn oil, for frying

lime wedges, to garnish

dip or salsa of choice, to serve

1 Place the potato in a small pan
and add water to cover. Add
a pinch of salt. Bring to a boil, then
reduce the heat, cover, and let simmer
for 10–15 minutes, or until softened.
Drain well, turn into a large bowl and
mash with a potato masher or fork
until smooth.

2 Meanwhile, place the scallions,
garlic, thyme, basil, and cilantro
in a mortar and pound with a pestle
until smooth. Add the herb paste to
the mashed potato with the crabmeat,
mustard, chili, egg, and pepper to
taste. Mix well, cover with plastic
wrap, and let chill in the refrigerator for
30 minutes.

3 Sprinkle flour onto a shallow
plate. Shape spoonfuls of the
crabmeat mixture into small balls with
your hands, then flatten slightly and
dust with flour, shaking off any excess.
Heat the oil in a skillet over high heat,
add the crab cakes, in batches, and
cook for 2–3 minutes on each side
until golden. Remove from the skillet
and drain on paper towels. Set aside to
cool to room temperature.

4 Arrange the crab cakes on a
serving dish and garnish with
lime wedges. Serve with a bowl of dip
or salsa.

crispy crab won tons

serves four

6 oz/175 g white crabmeat, flaked

1¾ oz/50 g canned water chestnuts, drained, rinsed, and chopped

1 small fresh red chili, chopped

1 scallion, chopped

1 tbsp cornstarch

1 tsp dry sherry

1 tsp light soy sauce

½ tsp lime juice

24 won ton skins

vegetable oil, for deep-frying

lime slices, to garnish

1 To make the filling, mix together the crabmeat, water chestnuts, chili, scallion, cornstarch, sherry, soy sauce, and lime juice.

2 Spread out the won ton skins on a counter and spoon one portion of the filling into the center of each won ton skin.

3 Dampen the edges of the won ton skins with a little water and fold them in half to form triangles. Fold the two pointed ends in toward the center, moisten with a little water to secure and then pinch together to seal to prevent the won tons unwrapping.

4 Heat the oil for deep-frying in a wok or deep-fat fryer to 350–375°F/180–190°C, or until a cube of bread browns in 30 seconds. Deep-fry the won tons, in batches, for 2–3 minutes, or until golden brown and crisp. Remove the won tons from the oil and let drain on paper towels.

5 Serve the won tons hot, garnished with lime slices.

COOK'S TIP

Handle won ton skins carefully because they can be easily damaged. Make sure that the won tons are sealed well and secured before deep-frying to prevent the filling coming out and the won tons unwrapping.

mussels in spiced batter

serves four

40 live large mussels in their shells

2 tbsp all-purpose flour

2 tbsp rice flour

½ tsp salt

1 tbsp dry unsweetened coconut

1 egg white

1 tbsp rice wine or dry sherry

2 tbsp water

1 small fresh red Thai chili, seeded and chopped

1 tbsp chopped fresh cilantro

corn oil, for deep-frying

lime wedges, to serve

1 Wash the mussels thoroughly by scrubbing or scraping the shells and pulling off any beards that are attached to them. Discard any with broken shells or any that refuse to close when tapped. Place the mussels in a large pan with just the water that clings to their shells and cook, covered, over high heat for 3–4 minutes, shaking the pan occasionally, until the mussels are opened. Drain well, let cool slightly, then remove from the shells. Discard any mussels that remain closed.

2 For the batter, sift the all-purpose flour, rice flour, and salt into a large bowl. Add the coconut, egg white, rice wine or sherry, and water and beat until well mixed and a batter forms. Stir the chili and cilantro into the batter.

COOK'S TIP

If you reserve the mussel shells, the cooked mussels can be replaced in them to serve.

3 Heat a 2-inch/5-cm depth of oil in a deep-fat fryer or large pan to 350–375°F/180–190°C, or until a cube of bread browns in 30 seconds. Holding the mussels with a fork, dip them quickly into the batter, then drop into the hot oil and deep-fry for 1–2 minutes, or until the mussels are crisp and golden brown.

4 Drain the mussels on paper towels and serve hot with lime wedges to squeeze over.

calamari

scant ¾ cup all-purpose flour

1 tsp salt

2 eggs

¾ cup club soda

1 lb/450 g squid

2½ cups vegetable oil,
    for deep-frying

TO GARNISH

lemon wedges

fresh parsley sprigs

COOK'S TIP

If you don't like the idea of
cleaning squid yourself, get
your store to do it. Sometimes,
squid is even sold already cut
into rings. Alternatively, you
could use prepared baby squid
for this dish.

1 Sift the flour and salt together
into a bowl. Add the eggs and
half the club soda and whisk together
until smooth. Gradually whisk in the
remaining club soda until the batter is
smooth. Set aside.

2 To prepare whole squid, hold the
body firmly and grasp the
tentacles just inside the body. Pull
firmly to remove the innards. Find the
transparent "backbone" and remove.
Grasp the wings on the outside of the
body and pull to remove the outer
skin. Trim the tentacles just below the
beak and set aside.

3 Wash the body and tentacles
under cold running water. Slice
the body across into ½-inch/1-cm rings.
Drain well on paper towels.

4 Meanwhile, fill a deep-fat fryer or
large pan about one-third full
with oil and heat to 350–375°F/
180–190°C, or until a cube of bread
browns in 30 seconds.

5 Dip the squid rings and tentacles
into the batter, a few at a time,
and drop into the hot oil. Deep-fry for
1–2 minutes, or until crisp and golden.
Drain on paper towels. Keep warm
while you cook the remaining squid.
Transfer to a large serving plate,
garnish with lemon wedges and
parsley sprigs, and serve at once.

fish cakes with sweet & sour sauce

makes sixteen

1 lb/450 g firm white fish, such as
hake, haddock, or cod, skinned
and coarsely chopped

1 tbsp Thai fish sauce

1 tbsp red curry paste

1 kaffir lime leaf, finely shredded

2 tbsp chopped fresh cilantro

1 egg

1 tsp brown sugar

salt

1½ oz/40 g green beans, thinly
sliced crosswise

vegetable oil, for cooking

SWEET & SOUR DIPPING SAUCE

4 tbsp sugar

1 tbsp cold water

3 tbsp white rice vinegar

2 small fresh hot red chilies,
finely chopped

1 tbsp Thai fish sauce

TO GARNISH

chili flower

scallion tassel

1 For the fish cakes, place the fish, fish sauce, curry paste, lime leaf, cilantro, egg, brown sugar, and salt to taste in a food processor. Process until smooth. Scrape into a bowl and stir in the green beans. Set aside.

2 To make the sauce, put the sugar, water, and vinegar into a small pan and heat gently until the sugar has dissolved. Bring to a boil, then reduce the heat and simmer the sauce for 2 minutes. Remove from the heat, stir in the chilies and fish sauce and set aside.

3 Heat a skillet with enough oil to cover the bottom generously. Divide the fish mixture into 16 little balls. Flatten the balls into little patties and cook in the hot oil for 1–2 minutes on each side, or until golden. Drain on paper towels, then garnish with the chili flower and scallion tassel. Serve hot with the dipping sauce.

COOK'S TIP

It isn't necessary to use the most
expensive cut of white fish in this
recipe because the other flavors
are very strong. Use whatever
is cheapest.

savory rice balls

serves four

scant 1 cup cooked rice or
   plain risotto

6 oz/175 g white crabmeat, flaked

3 scallions, finely chopped

2 tbsp mayonnaise

½ cup grated cheese, such as
   mozzarella, fontina, or Gruyère

pinch of cayenne pepper

1 tbsp finely chopped fresh parsley

2 eggs

oil, for deep-frying

2 tbsp all-purpose flour

bread crumbs, to coat

1 Combine the rice or risotto, crabmeat, scallions, mayonnaise, cheese, cayenne pepper, parsley, and 1 egg in a large bowl. Mix well. Cover the bowl with plastic wrap and let chill in the refrigerator for at least 2 hours or preferably overnight.

2 With wet hands, roll spoonfuls of the mixture into small balls. Cover and let chill for 30 minutes.

3 Heat the oil in a wok or large pan to 350–375°F/180–190°C, or until a cube of bread browns in 30 seconds.

4 Meanwhile, beat the remaining egg in a shallow dish. Gently roll the rice balls in flour, then quickly dip them in the beaten egg. Coat thoroughly and drain off any excess.

5 Roll the rice balls in bread crumbs. Press the bread crumbs in firmly but gently, then shake off any loose bread crumbs. Deep-fry in the hot oil for 5 minutes, or until crisp and golden. Drain well and serve either hot or cold.

grandma's chopped herring

serves four

4 rollmops, with onions

2 hard-cooked eggs

1 cooking apple

1 tbsp matzo meal or fine bread
  crumbs

1 Remove the skin from the
rollmops and discard. Chop the
herrings and place in a bowl.

2 Chop the onions and add to the
bowl. Shell the eggs and chop,
then peel, core, and chop the apple
and add both to the bowl.

3 Mix in the matzo meal or bread
crumbs and turn into a serving
dish. If not using immediately, cover
with plastic wrap and let chill until
10 minutes before required.

COOK'S TIP

Chopped herring goes
particularly well with thin
slices or fingers of rye bread
or pumpernickel.

devils & angels on horseback

makes thirty-two

DEVILS

8 rindless lean bacon slices

8 canned anchovies, drained

16 blanched almonds

16 no-soak prunes

ANGELS

8 rindless lean bacon slices

16 smoked oysters, drained
  if canned

1 Preheat the oven to 400°F/ 200°C. For the devils, cut each bacon slice lengthwise in half and gently stretch with the back of a knife. Cut each anchovy lengthwise in half. Wrap an anchovy half around each almond and press them into the cavity where the pits have been removed from the prunes. Wrap a strip of bacon around each prune and secure with a toothpick.

2 For the angels, cut each bacon slice lengthwise in half and gently stretch with the back of a knife. Wrap a bacon strip around each oyster and secure with a toothpick.

3 Place the devils and angels on a baking sheet and cook in the preheated oven for 10–15 minutes, or until sizzling hot and the bacon is cooked. Serve hot.

spicy seafood kabobs

makes eight

2 tsp grated fresh gingerroot

2 garlic cloves, finely chopped

2 fresh green chilies, seeded and
finely chopped

2 tbsp peanut or corn oil

3 lb 5 oz/1.5 kg angler fish fillet,
cut into 24 chunks

8 raw jumbo shrimp, peeled and
tails left intact

salt and pepper

SPICY SALSA

2 tomatoes

4 fresh Scotch bonnet chilies

4 fresh green jalapeño chilies,
seeded and finely chopped

2 tbsp chopped fresh cilantro

2 tbsp olive oil

1 tbsp red wine vinegar

salt

1 Mix together the ginger, garlic, green chilies and peanut or corn oil in a large, nonmetallic bowl. Add the angler fish chunks and shrimp and stir well to coat. Cover with plastic wrap and let marinate in the refrigerator for 1 hour.

2 Meanwhile, for the salsa, cut a small cross in the bottom of each tomato, place in a heatproof bowl, and pour over boiling water to cover. Let stand for 30 seconds until the skins start to peel back. Drain and, when cool enough to handle, peel.

3 Preheat the broiler to medium. Place the Scotch bonnet chilies on a baking sheet and cook under the hot broiler, turning frequently, until the skin blackens and blisters. Transfer to a plastic bag with tongs and tie the top.

4 Place the jalapeño chilies in a bowl. Scoop out and discard the tomato seeds, finely chop the flesh, and add to the bowl. Remove the Scotch bonnet chilies from the bag and peel away the skins. Halve them, discard the seeds, and finely chop the flesh. (Wear rubber gloves to protect your hands as they are very hot.) Add them to the bowl with the cilantro. Whisk the olive oil with the vinegar in a small bowl and season to taste with salt. Pour over the salsa, cover with plastic wrap and let chill in the refrigerator until required.

5 Preheat the broiler. Thread the seafood onto 8 skewers. Cook under the hot broiler, turning frequently, for 6–8 minutes, or until cooked and tender. Transfer to a serving dish, season to taste with salt and pepper, and serve with the salsa.

Vegetable Nibbles

Vegetables offer endless creative potential for party food in the rich variety of their natural, perfectly packaged forms. For instance, celery and chicory provide attractive hollows for herb-flavored cream cheese (see page 176), and bell pepper slices colorfully ring a sumptuous smoked salmon filling (see page 186), while mushrooms offer ideal cups for holding a delicious feta cheese and spinach stuffing (see page 188). However, the winning combination of sweet vegetable flesh within a crunchy savory coating is unmissable, as in Vegetable Fritters with Sweet & Sour Sauce (see page 194), Tofu Tempura (see page 202), and Mushroom Bites with Aïoli (see page 190). Some of these dishes are substantial enough to serve as a main event, but others are just tasty little treats—such as Chinese Potato Sticks (see page 207) or Chili Cornmeal Fries (see page 172)—to serve with drinks or as a snack.

flavored olives

makes 2 x scant 2½ cups

fresh herb sprigs, to serve

PROVENCAL OLIVES

3 dried red chilies

1 tsp black peppercorns

1¾ cups black niçoise olives in brine

2 lemon slices

1 tsp black mustard seeds

1 tbsp garlic-flavored olive oil

fruity extra virgin olive oil

CATALAN OLIVES

½ broiled red or orange bell pepper

scant 1 cup black olives in brine

1 cup pimiento-stuffed olives
    in brine

1 tbsp capers in brine, rinsed
    and drained

pinch of dried red pepper flakes

4 tbsp chopped fresh
    cilantro leaves

1 bay leaf

1 shallot, very finely chopped

1 tbsp fennel seeds, lightly crushed

1 tsp dried dill

fruity extra virgin olive oil

makes 1 x scant 2½ cups

GREEK OLIVES

½ large lemon

1¾ cups kalamata olives in brine,
    rinsed and drained

4 fresh thyme sprigs

fruity extra virgin olive oil

1 To make the Provençal olives, place the chilies and peppercorns in a mortar and lightly crush with a pestle. Drain and rinse the olives, then pat dry with paper towels. Put all the ingredients in a scant 2½-cup preserving jar. Pour in enough extra virgin olive oil to cover.

2 Seal the jar. Let stand for at least 10 days before serving, shaking the jar daily.

3 To make the Catalan olives, finely chop the bell pepper. Drain and rinse the olives, then pat dry with paper towels. Put all the ingredients into a scant 2½-cup preserving jar. Pour in enough oil to cover. Seal and let marinate as in Step 2.

4 To make the Greek olives, cut the lemon into 4 slices, then each slice into wedges. Slice each olive lengthwise on one side down to the stone. Put all the ingredients in a scant 2½-cup preserving jar. Pour in oil to cover. Seal and marinate as in Step 2.

5 To serve, spoon the olives into a serving bowl and garnish with herb sprigs.

corn patties

serves six

11½ oz/325 g canned corn
   kernels, drained

1 onion, finely chopped

1 tsp curry powder

1 garlic clove, crushed

1 tsp ground coriander

2 scallions, chopped

3 tbsp all-purpose flour

½ tsp baking powder

1 large egg

salt

4 tbsp corn oil

1 scallion, sliced, to garnish

VARIATION

Use garam masala in place of the ordinary curry powder, or ground cumin. Add a little finely chopped fresh gingerroot to the mixture for extra flavor.

1 Mash the drained corn lightly in a medium-size bowl. Add the onion, curry powder, garlic, coriander, scallions, flour, baking powder, and egg. Stir well and season to taste with salt.

2 Heat the oil in a skillet. Drop tablespoonfuls of the mixture carefully onto the hot oil, far enough apart for them not to run into each other as they cook.

3 Cook, turning each patty once, for 4–5 minutes, or until golden brown and firm to the touch. Take care not to turn them too soon, or they will break up in the skillet.

4 Remove the patties from the skillet with a slotted spoon and drain well on paper towels. Serve at once, garnished with the scallion.

chili cornmeal fries

serves four

2¼ cups instant cornmeal

2 tsp chili powder

1 tbsp olive oil or melted butter

salt and pepper

DIP

⅔ cup sour cream

1 tbsp chopped fresh parsley

COOK'S TIP

Easy-cook instant cornmeal is widely available in supermarkets and is quick to make. It will keep for up to 1 week in the refrigerator. The cornmeal can also be baked in a preheated oven at 400°F/200°C for 20 minutes.

1 Place 6 cups of water in a pan and bring to a boil. Add 2 teaspoons of salt, then add the instant cornmeal in a steady stream, stirring constantly.

2 Reduce the heat slightly and continue stirring for about 5 minutes. It is essential to stir the cornmeal, otherwise it will stick and burn. The cornmeal should have a thick consistency at this point and should be stiff enough to hold the spoon upright in the pan.

3 Add the chili powder to the cornmeal mixture and stir well. Season to taste with a little salt and pepper.

4 Spread the cornmeal out onto a cutting board or baking sheet to about 1½ inches/4 cm thick. Let cool and set.

5 Cut the cooled cornmeal mixture into thin wedges.

6 Heat the oil in a skillet. Add the cornmeal wedges and cook for 3–4 minutes on each side, or until golden and crisp. Alternatively, brush with melted butter and cook under a preheated hot broiler for 6–7 minutes, or until golden. Drain on paper towels.

7 Mix the sour cream with parsley and place in a bowl.

8 Serve the cornmeal fries with the sour cream and parsley dip.

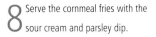

spiced corn & nut mix

serves four

2 tbsp vegetable oil

2 oz/55 g popcorn

2 oz/55 g butter

1 garlic clove, crushed

scant ½ cup unblanched almonds

scant ½ cup unsalted cashews

scant ½ cup unsalted peanuts

1 tsp Worcestershire sauce

1 tsp curry powder or paste

¼ tsp chili powder

⅓ cup seedless raisins

salt

VARIATION

Use a mixture of any unsalted nuts of your choice—walnuts, pecans, hazelnuts, Brazil nuts, macadamia nuts, and pine nuts. For a less fiery flavor, omit the curry and chili powder and add 1 teaspoon of cumin seeds, 1 teaspoon of ground coriander, and ½ teaspoon of paprika.

---

1 Heat the oil in a pan. Add the popcorn, stir well, then cover and cook over fairly high heat for 3–5 minutes, holding the pan lid firmly and shaking the pan frequently until the popping stops.

2 Turn the popped corn into a large dish, discarding any unpopped corn kernels.

3 Melt the butter in a skillet and add the garlic and nuts. Stir in the Worcestershire sauce, curry powder or paste, and chili powder and cook over medium heat, stirring frequently, for 2–3 minutes, or until the nuts are lightly toasted.

4 Remove the skillet from the heat and stir in the raisins and popped corn. Season to taste with salt and mix thoroughly. Transfer to a serving bowl and serve warm or cold.

celery & chicory boats

makes about thirty

1 lb/450 g cream cheese

4 scallions, finely chopped

4 tbsp chopped sun-dried tomatoes
   in oil

3 tbsp chopped fresh parsley

1 tbsp snipped fresh chives

generous 1 cup pimiento-stuffed
   olives, chopped

1 tbsp Tabasco sauce

2 heads chicory, separated
   into leaves

12 celery stalks

strips of red bell pepper, to garnish

1 Beat the cream cheese in a large bowl with a wooden spoon until smooth.

2 Stir in the scallions, sun-dried tomatoes, parsley, chives, olives, and Tabasco sauce and mix well.

3 Spoon the mixture into the hollows of the chicory leaves and celery stalks and arrange on a serving plate. Garnish with the strips of red bell pepper.

cheesy corn puffs

serves four

2 oz/55 g butter

⅔ cup water

½ cup all-purpose flour, seasoned
   with salt and pepper

1 egg, beaten

pinch of cayenne pepper or chili
   powder (optional)

1 oz/25 g cheese such as Emmental,
   Gruyère, or Cheddar, grated

1 tbsp canned corn kernels, sautéed
   onion, cooked mushrooms, or
   diced ham

oil, for deep-frying

1 To make the choux pastry, place the butter and water in a heavy-bottom pan and bring to a boil. Add the seasoned flour, all at once, and beat thoroughly until the mixture leaves the sides of the pan. Beat in the egg, a little at a time, until it has all been absorbed.

2 Season the mixture with cayenne pepper or chili powder, if using, and stir in the cheese and corn, onion, mushrooms, or ham.

3 Heat the oil in a preheated wok or deep pan. Gently drop small spoonfuls of the pastry into the oil. Cook until golden brown and puffed. Carefully remove from the oil and drain on a plate lined with paper towels. Serve at once.

cheese ball assortment

serves four

BLUE CHEESE BALLS

4 oz/115 g blue cheese, crumbled

½ cup sour cream

2 tbsp finely chopped scallions or
   snipped fresh chives

1 tbsp finely chopped celery

CREAM CHEESE BALLS

4 oz/115 g farmhouse cheese, such
   as Cheddar or Lancashire, grated

⅜ cup cream cheese

3 tbsp dry sherry or Martini

few drops of Worcestershire sauce

2 tbsp finely chopped scallions or
   snipped fresh chives

1 tbsp finely chopped celery

FETA CHEESE BALLS

4 oz/115 g feta cheese (drained
   weight), crumbled

4 oz/115 g butter, softened

½ tsp paprika

2 tbsp finely chopped fresh herbs

TO SERVE

chopped nuts, shredded ham,
   minced green or red bell pepper,
   chopped celery, finely chopped
   fresh herbs

1 To make the Blue Cheese Balls, mash the cheese in a bowl and mix with the sour cream to make a smooth paste. Add the scallions or chives and celery. With wet hands, take small spoonfuls of the mixture and form into balls. Arrange on a plate, cover with plastic wrap, and let chill.

2 To make the Cream Cheese Balls, mash the farmhouse cheese with the cream cheese in a bowl to make a smooth paste. Season with sherry, or Martini, and Worcestershire sauce. Fold in the scallions, or chives, and celery. Shape and let chill as in Step 1.

3 To make the Feta Cheese Balls, mash the cheese with the butter in a bowl to make a smooth paste. Season with paprika and herbs, shape, and let chill as in Step 1.

4 Roll any of the cheese balls in chopped nuts, shredded ham, minced green or red bell pepper, celery, or fresh herbs, or use a variety of different coatings.

toasted nibbles

serves four

½ cup ricotta cheese

4 oz/115 g Gloucester or Cheddar
   cheese, finely grated

2 tsp chopped fresh parsley

pepper

scant ½ cup chopped mixed nuts

3 tbsp chopped fresh mixed herbs,
   such as parsley, chives,
   marjoram, lovage, and chervil

2 tbsp mild paprika

fresh herb sprigs, to garnish

1 Combine the ricotta with the Gloucester or Cheddar cheese. Add the parsley, season with pepper, and mix together until thoroughly combined.

2 Form the mixture into small balls and place on a plate. Cover and let chill in the refrigerator for about 20 minutes, until they are firm.

3 Preheat the broiler. Sprinkle the chopped nuts onto a baking sheet and place them under the hot broiler until lightly browned. Take care because they can easily burn. Remove from the broiler and set aside to cool.

4 Place the nuts, mixed herbs, and paprika into 3 separate small bowls. Remove the cheese balls from the refrigerator and divide into 3 equal piles. Roll 1 quantity of the cheese balls in the nuts, 1 quantity in the herbs, and 1 quantity in the paprika.

5 Arrange the coated cheese balls alternately on a large serving platter. Cover and let chill in the refrigerator until ready to serve, and then garnish with sprigs of fresh herbs.

cheese & apricot morsels

makes twenty

1 cup cream cheese

6 tbsp milk

4 oz/115 g sharp Cheddar cheese, finely grated

salt and pepper

1 lb 12 oz/800 g canned apricot halves in juice, drained

TO GARNISH

about 20 walnut pieces

paprika

1 Beat the cream cheese in a bowl with a wooden spoon until softened. Gradually beat in the milk and cheese. Season to taste with salt and pepper.

2 Spoon the cheese mixture into a pastry bag fitted with a ½-inch/ 1-cm star tip. Pipe swirls of the mixture into the hollow of each apricot half.

3 Arrange the filled apricot halves in a serving dish, then top each with a piece of walnut and dust lightly with a little paprika, to garnish.

stuffed grape leaves

serves twelve

- scant 1¾ cups long-grain rice
- 1 lb/450 g grape leaves, rinsed if preserved in brine
- 2 onions, finely chopped
- 1 bunch scallions, finely chopped
- 1 bunch fresh parsley, finely chopped
- 2 tbsp fresh mint, finely chopped
- 1 tbsp fennel seeds
- 1 tsp crushed dried chilies
- finely grated rind of 2 lemons
- 1 cup olive oil
- salt
- 2½ cups boiling water
- lemon wedges, to garnish
- Tzatziki (see page 15), to serve

1 Bring a large pan of lightly salted water to a boil. Add the rice and return to a boil. Reduce the heat and let simmer for 15 minutes, or until tender.

2 Meanwhile, if using preserved grape leaves, place them in a heatproof bowl and pour over boiling water to cover. Set aside to soak for 10 minutes. If using fresh grape leaves, bring a pan of water to a boil, add the grape leaves, then reduce the heat and let simmer for 10 minutes.

3 Drain the rice and, while still hot, mix with the onions, scallions, parsley, mint, fennel seeds, chilies, lemon rind, and 3 tablespoons of the oil in a large bowl. Season to taste with salt.

4 Drain the grape leaves well. Spread out 1 leaf, vein-side up, on a counter. Place a generous teaspoonful of the rice mixture on the leaf near the stalk. Fold the stalk end over the filling, fold in the sides and roll up the leaf. Repeat until all the filling has been used. There may be some grape leaves left over—you can use them to line a serving platter, if wished.

5 Place the packages in a large, heavy-bottom pan in a single layer (you may need to use 2 pans). Spoon over the remaining oil, then add the boiling water. Cover the packages with an inverted heatproof plate to keep them below the surface of the water, cover the pan, and let simmer for 1 hour.

6 Allow the packages to cool to room temperature in the pan, then transfer to a serving platter with a slotted spoon. Garnish with lemon wedges and serve with Tzatziki.

stuffed mushrooms

serves four

1 lb/450 g white mushrooms

3 garlic cloves

2 tbsp minced onion

6 oz/175 g butter

½ cup fresh white bread crumbs

1 tsp chopped fresh parsley, plus
    extra to garnish

1 tbsp grated Parmesan cheese

1 Preheat the oven to 350°F/
180°C.

2 Remove the stems from the mushrooms and finely chop the stems. Finely chop 2 garlic cloves. Mix with the onion and mushroom stems.

3 Melt half the butter in a heavy-bottom skillet over medium heat. Cook the mushroom stems, onion, and garlic for 3 minutes, or until softened. In a small bowl, combine the bread crumbs, parsley, and cheese. Stir into the hot onion mixture. Place a small spoonful in each mushroom cap.

4 Melt the remaining butter in a small pan. Crush the remaining garlic clove and toss in the butter for 2 minutes. Pour half into a shallow, ovenproof dish.

5 Arrange the stuffed mushroom caps in the dish and pour over the remaining flavored butter. Bake in the preheated oven for 20 minutes. Serve at once, garnished with parsley.

stuffed tomatoes

serves four

2 tbsp butter, melted

2 tbsp pine nuts

8 water chestnuts, sliced

generous ½ cup long-grain rice

1 cup chicken stock

4 medium or 8 small tomatoes

fresh chive lengths, to garnish

1 Melt the butter in a pan over medium heat. Toss in the pine nuts, water chestnuts, and rice. Stir to coat.

2 Add the stock, cover, and cook gently for 20 minutes, or until all the liquid is absorbed and the rice is tender. Let cool.

3 Slice the top off the tomatoes and scoop out the seeds. Fill with the cooked rice mixture and serve at room temperature, garnished with chives.

stuffed bell peppers

serves four

4 red, yellow, or green bell peppers

½ cup cream cheese

½ tsp lemon juice

2 oz/55 g smoked salmon, diced or
minced

salt and pepper

VARIATION

Add a little chopped fresh dill or
snipped fresh chives to the
cheese mixture and garnish with
dill or herb sprigs. Use smoked
trout in place of smoked salmon
or try diced lean ham instead.

---

1 Cut a thick slice off the top of the
bell peppers and carefully remove
all the seeds.

2 Beat the cream cheese with the
lemon juice in a bowl with a
wooden spoon until light and smooth.
Add the smoked salmon and blend
thoroughly. Season to taste with salt
and pepper.

3 Fill the bell peppers with the
cheese mixture, packing it in
gently. Cover with plastic wrap and let
chill in the refrigerator for 3–4 hours.

4 To serve the Stuffed Bell Peppers,
unwrap and cut into thin slices
horizontally. Arrange overlapping slices
on a serving platter and serve.

spinach stuffed mushrooms

serves four

2 oz/55 g feta cheese
(drained weight)

12 large mushrooms

3 tbsp dry white wine

3 tbsp water

1 shallot, chopped

1 fresh thyme sprig, finely chopped

2 tsp lemon juice

1 tbsp butter

salt and pepper

2 tsp olive oil

1 garlic clove, finely chopped

3 ¼ cups fresh spinach,
coarse stalks removed and
leaves chopped

COOK'S TIP

There is no need to peel
mushrooms unless their skin is
leathery or discolored. Just
carefully wipe off the dirt with
damp paper towels.

1 Preheat the oven to 350°F/
180°C. Crumble the feta and set
aside. Remove the stems from the
mushrooms and finely chop the stems.

2 Pour the wine and water into a
wide pan and add half the shallot
and the thyme. Bring to a boil, then
reduce the heat and let simmer for
2 minutes. Add the mushroom caps,
smooth side down, and sprinkle over
the lemon juice. Cover, let simmer for
6 minutes, then remove the
mushrooms and place on a plate to
drain. Return the liquid to a boil, add
the mushroom stems and butter, and
season to taste with salt. Cook for
6 minutes, or until the liquid has been
absorbed. Transfer to a bowl.

3 Heat the oil in a clean pan. Add
the remaining shallot, garlic, and
spinach and sprinkle with a little salt.
Cook over medium heat, stirring, for
3 minutes, or until all the liquid has
evaporated. Stir the spinach mixture
into the mushroom stems, season to
taste with pepper, then gently stir in
the reserved feta.

4 Divide the spinach mixture
between the mushroom caps.
Place them in a single layer in an
ovenproof dish and bake in the
preheated oven for 15–20 minutes,
or until golden. Serve warm.

mushroom bites with aïoli

serves four

4 oz/115 g fresh white bread

2 tbsp freshly grated
   Parmesan cheese

1 tsp paprika

2 egg whites

8 oz/225 g white mushrooms

AIOLI

4 garlic cloves, crushed

2 egg yolks

1 cup extra virgin olive oil

salt and pepper

1 Preheat the oven to 375°F/
190°C. To make the aïoli, put the
garlic in a bowl, add a pinch of salt,
and mash with the back of a spoon.
Add the egg yolks and beat with an
electric whisk for 30 seconds, or until
creamy. Start beating in the oil, one
drop at a time. As the mixture starts to
thicken, add the oil in a steady stream,
beating constantly. Season to taste
with salt and pepper, cover the bowl
with plastic wrap, and let chill in the
refrigerator until required.

2 Line a large baking sheet with
parchment paper. Grate the bread
into bread crumbs and place them in a
bowl with the Parmesan cheese and
paprika. Lightly whisk the egg whites
in a separate clean bowl, then dip each
mushroom first into the egg whites,
then into the bread crumbs, and place
on the prepared baking sheet.

3 Bake in the preheated oven for
15 minutes, or until the coating is
crisp and golden. Serve at once with
the aïoli.

bite-size bhajis

serves four

2 heaping tbsp gram flour

½ tsp ground turmeric

½ tsp ground cumin seeds

1 tsp garam masala

pinch of cayenne pepper

1 egg

1 large onion, cut into fourths
    and sliced

salt

1 tbsp chopped fresh cilantro

3 tbsp fresh bread crumbs (optional)

vegetable oil, for deep-frying

fresh cilantro leaves, to garnish

SAUCE

1 tsp ground coriander seeds

1½ tsp ground cumin seeds

1 cup plain yogurt

salt and pepper

COOK'S TIP

Make sure that the skillet and all
the utensils are properly dried
before use. Do not let any water
come into contact with the hot
oil or the oil will spit and splutter,
which could be dangerous.

1 Put the gram flour into a large
bowl and mix in the turmeric,
cumin seeds, garam masala, and
cayenne pepper. Make a well in the
center and add the egg. Stir to form a
sticky mixture. Add the onion and
sprinkle in a little salt. Add the fresh
cilantro and stir. If the mixture is not
stiff enough, stir in the bread crumbs.

2 Heat the oil for deep-frying over
medium heat until fairly hot—it
should just be starting to smoke.

3 Push teaspoonfuls of the mixture
into the oil with a second
teaspoon to form fairly round balls.
Cook in batches of 8–10, stirring so
that they brown evenly. Drain on paper
towels and keep them warm in the
oven until ready to serve.

4 For the sauce, toast the spices in
a dry skillet. Remove from the
heat. Stir in the yogurt and salt and
pepper to taste. Transfer to a serving
dish. Serve the bhajis with the sauce.

celery with olive cheese filling

serves four

12 celery stalks

1 cup cream cheese

⅓ cup black or green olives, pitted and finely chopped

2 oz/55 g canned or bottled pimientos, drained and finely chopped

2 scallions, finely chopped

1 tbsp finely chopped fresh parsley

2 tsp Tabasco or hot pepper sauce (optional)

VARIATION

You could use pimiento-stuffed green olives instead of the olives and pimientos separately, or try roasted bell peppers in jars, available from supermarkets.

1 Trim the celery stalks, removing all the leaves and any coarse strings.

2 Beat the cream cheese in a bowl with a wooden spoon until soft and smooth. Add all the other ingredients and mix well.

3 Spoon or pipe the cream cheese into the celery stalks. Cut the stalks into 2-inch/5-cm pieces, arrange on a serving dish, and serve.

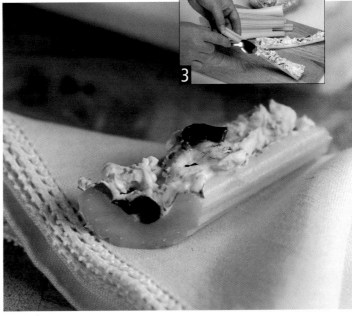

vegetable fritters with sweet & sour sauce

serves four

¾ cup whole-wheat flour

pinch of salt

pinch of cayenne pepper

4 tsp olive oil

12 tbsp cold water

3½ oz/100 g broccoli florets

3½ oz/100 g cauliflower florets

1¾ oz/50 g snow peas

1 large carrot, cut into thin sticks

1 red bell pepper, seeded and sliced

2 egg whites

vegetable oil, for deep-frying

SAUCE

⅔ cup pineapple juice

⅔ cup vegetable stock

2 tbsp wine vinegar

2 tbsp brown sugar

2 tsp cornstarch

2 scallions, chopped

1 Sift the flour and salt into a large bowl and add the cayenne pepper. Make a well in the center and gradually beat in the oil and cold water to form a smooth batter.

2 Cook the vegetables in a large pan of boiling water for 5 minutes. Drain well.

3 Whisk the egg whites in a clean, dry bowl until peaks form, then fold into the batter.

4 Dip the vegetables into the batter, turning to coat well. Drain off any excess batter. Heat the oil for deep-frying in a deep-fat fryer or heavy-bottom pan to 350–375°F/ 180–190°C, or until a cube of bread browns in 30 seconds. Deep-fry the vegetables, in batches, for 1–2 minutes, or until golden. Remove from the oil with a slotted spoon and drain on paper towels.

5 Place all the ingredients for the sauce in a pan and bring to a boil, stirring. Cook until thickened and clear. Serve with the fritters.

mixed vegetable fritters

serves four

generous 1 cup all-purpose flour

½ tsp baking powder

pinch of salt

1 egg

½ cup milk

½ tsp Tabasco sauce (optional)

1 large onion

1 large zucchini

1 small eggplant

1 small cauliflower

4 oz/115 g white mushrooms

oil, for deep-frying

lemon wedges, to garnish

garlicky tomato sauce, to serve

1 To prepare the batter, combine the dry ingredients in a large mixing bowl. Add the egg, beating well to eliminate lumps. Gradually add the milk, stirring constantly. Add the Tabasco sauce, if using.

2 Thickly slice the onion and separate into rings. Cut the zucchini and eggplant into thin sticks. Cut the cauliflower into florets. Trim the stems of the mushrooms level with the caps.

3 Heat the oil in a wok or deep pan to 350–375°F/180–190°C, or until a cube of bread browns in 30 seconds. Dip the vegetables into the batter, then lift out and drain any excess back into the bowl. Gently drop into the wok and cook until golden brown. Carefully remove from the oil with a slotted spoon and drain on a plate lined with paper towels.

4 Serve hot, garnished with lemon wedges and accompanied by a garlicky tomato sauce for dipping.

fritters with garlic sauce

serves four

1 lb 2 oz/500 g waxy
  potatoes, diced
4½ oz/125 g Parmesan cheese,
  freshly grated
vegetable oil, for deep-frying
SAUCE
2 tbsp butter
1 onion, halved and sliced
2 garlic cloves, crushed
2½ tbsp all-purpose flour
1¼ cups milk
1 tbsp chopped fresh parsley
BATTER
5 tbsp all-purpose flour
1 small egg
⅔ cup milk

1 To make the sauce, melt the butter in a pan and cook the onion and garlic over low heat, stirring frequently, for 2–3 minutes. Add the flour and cook, stirring constantly, for 1 minute.

2 Remove from the heat and stir in the milk and parsley. Return to the heat and bring to a boil. Keep the sauce warm.

3 Meanwhile, cook the potatoes in a pan of boiling water for 5–10 minutes, or until just firm. Do not overcook or they will fall apart.

4 Drain the potatoes and toss them in the Parmesan cheese. If the potatoes are still slightly wet, the cheese will stick to them and coat them well.

5 To make the batter, place the flour in a mixing bowl and gradually beat in the egg and milk until smooth. Dip the potato cubes into the batter to coat them.

6 Heat the oil in a deep-fat fryer or large pan to 350–375°F/ 180–190°C, or until a cube of bread browns in 30 seconds. Add the fritters, in batches if necessary, and cook for 3–4 minutes, or until golden.

7 Remove the fritters with a slotted spoon and drain well. Transfer them to a warmed serving bowl and serve the fritters at once with the garlic sauce.

zucchini & thyme fritters

makes sixteen–thirty

scant ⅔ cup self-rising flour

2 eggs, beaten

¼ cup milk

10½ oz/300 g zucchini

2 tbsp finely chopped fresh thyme

salt and pepper

1 tbsp oil

VARIATION

Try adding ½ teaspoon of crushed dried chilies to the batter in Step 4 for spicier-tasting fritters.

---

1 Sift the flour into a large mixing bowl and make a well in the center. Add the eggs to the well. Using a wooden spoon, gradually draw in the flour.

2 Slowly add the milk to the mixture, stirring constantly until a thick batter is formed. Set aside.

3 Wash the zucchini, then grate them over a paper towel placed in a bowl to absorb some of the juices.

4 Add the zucchini, thyme, and salt and pepper to taste to the batter and mix thoroughly.

5 Heat the oil in a large, heavy-bottom skillet. Taking a tablespoon of the batter for a medium-size fritter or half a tablespoon of batter for a smaller-size fritter, spoon the mixture into the hot oil, and cook the fritters, in batches, for 3–4 minutes on each side.

6 Remove the fritters with a slotted spoon and drain them thoroughly on paper towels. Keep each batch of fritters warm in the oven while making the remainder. Transfer to warmed serving plates and serve hot.

tofu tempura

serves four

4½ oz/125 g baby zucchini

4½ oz/125 g baby carrots

4½ oz/125 g baby corn

4½ oz/125 g baby leeks

2 baby eggplants

8 oz/225 g firm tofu (drained
    weight)

vegetable oil, for deep-frying

julienne strips of carrot, fresh
    gingerroot, and leek, to garnish

noodles, to serve

BATTER

2 egg yolks

1¼ cups water

scant 1½ cups all-purpose flour

DIPPING SAUCE

5 tbsp mirin or dry sherry

5 tbsp Japanese soy sauce

2 tsp honey

1 garlic clove, crushed

1 tsp grated fresh gingerroot

1 Cut the zucchini and carrots in half lengthwise. Trim the baby corn. Trim the leeks at both ends. Cut the eggplants into quarters lengthwise. Cut the tofu into 1-inch/2.5-cm cubes.

2 To make the batter, mix the egg yolks with the water in a large mixing bowl. Sift in 1 cup of the flour and beat with a balloon whisk to form a thick batter. Don't worry if there are some lumps. Heat the oil in a wok or large pan to 350–375°F/180–190°C, or until a cube of bread browns in 30 seconds.

3 Place the remaining flour on a large plate. Toss the prepared vegetables and tofu in the flour until lightly coated.

4 Dip the tofu in the batter and deep-fry for 2–3 minutes, or until lightly golden. Drain on paper towels and keep warm.

5 Dip the vegetables in the batter and deep-fry, in batches, for 3–4 minutes, or until golden. Drain and place on a warmed serving plate.

6 To make the dipping sauce, mix all the ingredients together. Serve with the vegetables and tofu, accompanied with noodles and garnished with julienne strips of fresh vegetables.

indonesian peanut fritters

makes twenty

scant ½ cup rice flour

½ tsp baking powder

½ tsp ground turmeric

½ tsp ground coriander

¼ tsp ground cumin

1 garlic clove, finely chopped

scant ½ cup unsalted peanuts,
   crushed

½–⅔ cup coconut milk

salt

peanut oil, for frying

1 Combine the rice flour, baking powder, turmeric, coriander, cumin, garlic, and peanuts in a bowl. Gradually stir in enough coconut milk to make a smooth, thin batter. Season to taste with salt.

2 Pour the oil into a heavy-bottom skillet to a depth of about ½ inch/1 cm and heat over high heat until hot. Add tablespoonfuls of the batter to the skillet, spacing them well apart, and cook until the tops have just set and the undersides are golden. Turn the fritters over and cook for 1 minute, or until the second side is golden. Remove with a spatula, drain on paper towels, and keep warm while cooking the remaining fritters. Serve at once.

VARIATION

Use 1½ teaspoons of a spice mix, such as garam masala, in place of the individual spices. Try using unsalted cashews instead of peanuts.

3 Alternatively, transfer the fritters to wire racks to cool, then store in an airtight container. When ready to serve, place them on baking sheets and reheat in a preheated oven at 350°F/180°C for 10 minutes.

black bean nachos

serves four

1⅓ cups dried black beans, or
    canned black beans, drained
1½–2 cups grated cheese, such as
    Cheddar, fontina, romano, or
    Asiago, or a combination
about ¼ tsp cumin seeds or
    ground cumin
about 4 tbsp sour cream
thinly sliced pickled jalapeño chilies
    (optional)
1 tbsp chopped fresh cilantro
handful of shredded lettuce
tortilla chips, to serve

VARIATION

To add a meaty flavor, spoon
chopped and browned chorizo
sausage on top of the beans
before sprinkling over the cheese
and baking—the combination is
excellent. Finely chopped leftover
cooked meat can also be added
in this way.

1 If using dried black beans, soak
   the beans overnight, then drain.
Place in a pan, cover with water, and
bring to a boil. Boil for 10 minutes,
then reduce the heat and let
simmer for 1½ hours, or until tender.
Drain well.

2 Preheat the oven to 375°F/
   190°C. Spread the beans in a
shallow, ovenproof dish, then sprinkle
the cheese over the top. Sprinkle with
cumin to taste.

3 Bake in the preheated oven for
   10–15 minutes, or until the beans
are cooked through and the cheese is
bubbly and melted.

4 Remove from the oven and spoon
   the sour cream on top. Add the
chilies, if using, and sprinkle with
cilantro and lettuce.

5 Arrange the tortilla chips around
   the beans, placing them in the
mixture. Serve the nachos at once.

crunchy potato skins

serves four

4 potatoes, cooked in their skins

2 lean bacon slices

4 oz/115 g blue cheese, crumbled

oil, for deep-frying

soured cream or plain yogurt,
  to garnish

1 Cut the potatoes into quarters. Scoop out the soft inside, leaving a lining about ¼ inch/5 mm thick.

2 Preheat the broiler, then broil the bacon until crisp. Transfer to a cutting board and cut into small strips. Combine the blue cheese and bacon in a small mixing bowl.

3 Heat the oil in a wok or deep pan to 350–375°F/180–190°C, or until a cube of bread browns in 30 seconds. Carefully drop the potato skins into the oil and deep-fry for 3–4 minutes, or until crisp and golden. Remove and drain well on paper towels.

4 Arrange the potato skins on a large plate and fill each with a spoonful of the bacon and cheese mixture, piling it high so that it is almost overflowing. Garnish with a teaspoon of sour cream or plain yogurt and serve at once.

COOK'S TIP

Garnish the potato skins with a sprinkling of snipped fresh chives.

205

buttered herby new potatoes

serves four

12 small new potatoes

4 oz/115 g butter

2 tbsp finely chopped
	fresh rosemary

salt and pepper

fresh rosemary sprigs, to garnish

VARIATION

Add 1–2 crushed garlic cloves
to the rosemary butter.

---

1 Boil the potatoes in a large pan of lightly salted water until just tender. Drain well.

2 Melt the butter in a large, heavy-bottom skillet. Add the rosemary and the potatoes and mix well. Cook over medium–high heat, stirring frequently, for 5 minutes, or until the potatoes are thoroughly coated in the rosemary butter and are starting to brown.

3 Arrange the potatoes on large serving platters and season with salt and pepper to taste. Garnish with rosemary sprigs and serve at once.

chinese potato sticks

serves four

1 lb 7 oz/650 g potatoes

½ cup vegetable oil

1 fresh red chili, seeded
    and halved

1 small onion, quartered

2 garlic cloves, halved

2 tbsp soy sauce

pinch of salt

1 tsp wine vinegar

1 tbsp sea salt

pinch of chili powder

1 Peel the potatoes and cut into thin slices lengthwise. Cut the slices into short, thin sticks.

2 Bring a pan of water to a boil and blanch the potato sticks for 2 minutes. Drain, rinse under cold running water, and drain well again. Pat the potato sticks thoroughly dry with paper towels.

3 Heat the oil in a preheated wok until it is almost smoking. Add the chili, onion, and garlic and stir-fry for 30 seconds. Remove and discard the chili, onion, and garlic.

4 Add the potato sticks to the oil and stir-fry for 3–4 minutes, or until golden brown.

5 Add the soy sauce, salt, and vinegar to the wok, reduce the heat and stir-fry for 1 minute, or until the potatoes are crisp.

6 Remove the potatoes with a slotted spoon and let drain on paper towels.

7 Transfer the potato sticks to a serving dish, sprinkle with the sea salt and chili powder, and serve.

VARIATION

Sprinkle other flavorings over the cooked potato sticks, such as curry powder, or serve with a chili dip.

potato kibbeh

serves four

1 cup bulgur wheat

12 oz/350 g mealy potatoes, diced

2 small eggs

2 tbsp butter, melted

pinch of ground cumin

pinch of ground coriander

pinch of grated nutmeg

salt and pepper

vegetable oil, for deep-frying

STUFFING

¾ cup fresh ground lamb

1 small onion, chopped

1 tbsp pine nuts

2 tbsp no-soak dried
   apricots, chopped

pinch of grated nutmeg

pinch of ground cinnamon

1 tbsp chopped fresh cilantro

2 tbsp lamb stock

1 Put the bulgur wheat in a heatproof bowl and pour in boiling water to cover. Set aside to soak for 30 minutes, or until the water has been absorbed and the bulgur wheat has swollen.

2 Meanwhile, cook the diced potatoes in a pan of boiling water for 10 minutes or until cooked through. Drain and mash until smooth.

3 Add the bulgur wheat to the mashed potatoes with the eggs, butter, cumin, coriander, and nutmeg. Mix well and season to taste with salt and pepper.

4 To make the stuffing, dry-fry the lamb in a heavy-bottom skillet for 5 minutes. Add the onion and cook for an additional 2–3 minutes. Add the remaining stuffing ingredients and cook for 5 minutes, or until the stock has been absorbed. Let the mixture cool slightly, then divide into 8 portions. Roll each one into a ball.

5 Divide the potato mixture into 8 portions. Flatten each into a circle. Place a portion of the stuffing in the center of each circle. Shape the potato mixture around the stuffing to encase it.

6 Heat the oil in a deep-fat fryer or large pan to 350–375°F/ 180–190°C, or until a cube of bread browns in 30 seconds. Cook the kibbeh for 5–7 minutes, or until golden brown. Drain well on paper towels and serve at once.

paprika chips

serves four

2 large potatoes

3 tbsp olive oil

½ tsp paprika

salt

VARIATION

You could use curry powder or
any other spice to flavor the
chips instead of the paprika,
if you prefer.

---

1 Preheat the barbecue or broiler.
Using a sharp knife, slice the
potatoes very thinly so that they are
almost transparent. Rinse, then drain
the potato slices thoroughly and pat
dry with paper towels.

2 Heat the oil in a large skillet and
add the paprika, stirring
constantly to ensure that the paprika
doesn't catch and burn.

3 Add the potato slices to the skillet
and cook them in a single layer
for 5 minutes, or until just starting to
curl slightly at the edges.

4 Remove the potato slices from
the skillet using a slotted spoon
and transfer them to paper towels to
drain thoroughly.

5 Thread the potato slices onto
presoaked wooden skewers.

6 Sprinkle the potato slices with a
little salt and barbecue over
medium coals or cook under the
hot broiler, turning frequently, for
10 minutes, or until the potato slices
start to crisp. Sprinkle with a little more
salt, if wished, and serve at once.

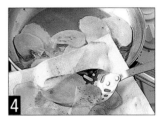

homemade oven fries

serves four

1 lb/450 g potatoes, peeled

2 tbsp corn oil

salt and pepper

1 Preheat the oven to 400°F/200°C.

2 Cut the potatoes into thick, even-size fries. Rinse them under cold running water and then dry well on a clean dish towel. Put in a bowl, add the oil, and toss together until thoroughly coated.

3 Spread the fries on a baking sheet and cook in the preheated oven for 40–45 minutes, turning once, until golden. Add salt and pepper to taste and serve hot.

Breads

Bread provides the perfect hand-held vehicle for all manner of savory ingredients, piled on top or encased between layers. Pizzas never fail to please, and here we have them in many guises, from traditional dough-based pizzas to fast-food options using English muffins and mini pita breads. Variations on toast are also inspiring, from bubbling Bruschetta (see page 214) to tasty Egg & Tapenade or Basil Zucchini Toasties (see pages 233 and 236), as well as crunchy Goat Cheese & Chive Croutons (see page 245). But there are some good homemade bread recipes too, like the olive-flavored Mini Focaccia (see page 238) or Sun-Dried Tomato Rolls (see page 239) for an authentic taste of the Mediterranean. For something simple yet eye-catching for a special occasion, serve the Ham & Parmesan Pinwheels (see page 251) or the Anchovy Bites (see page 252).

bruschetta

makes thirty

3 thin ciabatta loaves or baguettes

½ cup green pesto

½ cup red pesto

1 lb/450 g mozzarella cheese, diced

2 tsp dried oregano

pepper

3 tbsp olive oil

VARIATION

Use goat cheese, crumbled or thinly sliced, or provolone cheese, thinly sliced, in place of the mozzarella cheese. Sprinkle the bruschetta with a handful of torn fresh basil leaves instead of the dried oregano before baking.

---

1 Preheat the oven to 425°F/220°C and the broiler to medium. Slice the loaves diagonally and discard the crusty ends. Toast the slices on both sides under the hot broiler until golden.

2 Spread one side of each slice of toast with either green or red pesto and top with the mozzarella. Sprinkle with the oregano and season to taste with pepper.

3 Place the bruschetta on a large baking sheet and drizzle with the oil. Bake in the preheated oven for 5 minutes, or until the cheese has melted and is bubbling. Remove the bruschetta from the oven and let stand for 5 minutes before serving.

garlic bread

serves four

5½ oz/150 g butter, softened

3 garlic cloves, crushed

2 tbsp chopped fresh parsley

pepper

1 large or 2 small sticks of
 French bread

VARIATION

Alternatively, bake the garlic
bread in a preheated oven
at 375°F/190°C for
15 minutes.

---

1 Preheat the grill. Mix the butter, garlic, and parsley together in a bowl until well combined. Season to taste with pepper.

2 Cut the French bread into thick slices. Spread the garlic and parsley butter over 1 side of each slice and reassemble the loaf on a large sheet of thick foil.

3 Wrap the bread well in foil and grill over hot coals for about 10–15 minutes, or until the butter melts and the bread is piping hot.

4 Serve as an accompaniment to a wide range of dishes.

piperade

serves four–six

2 tbsp olive oil

1 large onion, finely chopped

1 large red bell pepper, seeded
and sliced

1 large yellow bell pepper, seeded
and sliced

1 large green bell pepper, seeded
and sliced

8 large eggs

salt and pepper

2 tomatoes, seeded and chopped

2 tbsp finely chopped fresh
flatleaf parsley

fresh flatleaf parsley sprigs,
to garnish

4–6 slices thick country-style bread,
toasted, to serve

1 Heat the oil in a heavy-bottom skillet over medium–high heat. Add the onion and bell peppers, reduce the heat, and cook, stirring occasionally, for 15–20 minutes, or until softened.

2 Place the eggs in a mixing bowl and whisk until well blended. Season to taste with salt and pepper. Set aside.

3 When the bell peppers are soft, pour the eggs into the skillet and cook, stirring constantly, over very low heat until they are almost set but still creamy. Remove from the heat.

4 Stir in the tomatoes and chopped parsley. Taste and adjust the seasoning, if necessary. Place the slices of toast on individual serving plates and spoon the eggs and vegetables on top. Garnish with parsley sprigs and serve at once.

COOK'S TIP

To make this dish more substantial, serve with thickly cut slices of Serrano ham from Spain or prosciutto from Italy. The salty taste of both meats contrasts well with the sweetness of the bell peppers.

olive & tomato bruschetta

serves four

½ cup extra virgin olive oil

1 small oval-shaped loaf of white
   bread (ciabatta or bloomer),
   cut into ½-inch/1-cm slices

4 tomatoes, seeded and diced

6 fresh basil leaves, torn

salt and pepper

8 black olives, pitted and chopped

1 large garlic clove, peeled
   and halved

1 Pour half the oil into a shallow dish and place the bread in it. Let stand for 1–2 minutes, then turn and leave for an additional 2 minutes. The bread should be thoroughly saturated in oil.

2 Meanwhile, put the tomatoes into a mixing bowl. Sprinkle the basil leaves over the tomatoes. Season to taste with salt and pepper and add the olives. Pour over the remaining oil and let marinate while you toast the bruschetta.

3 Preheat the broiler to medium. Place the bread on the broiler rack and cook for 2 minutes on each side, or until golden and crisp.

4 Remove the bread from the broiler and arrange in a plate.

5 Rub the cut edge of the garlic halves over the surface of the bruschetta, then top each slice with a spoonful of the tomato mixture. Serve at once.

fresh figs with gorgonzola

serves four

4 fresh figs

8 slices French baguette, ciabatta, or bloomer

4 oz/115 g Gorgonzola or other strong blue cheese, sliced or crumbled

1 Cut the figs into thin slices. Heat the broiler to medium. Place the bread on the broiler rack and toast until golden on 1 side. Remove the rack.

2 Turn the bread over and top with cheese, making sure that it covers each slice right to the edge.

3 Arrange the figs on top of the cheese.

4 Return the rack to the broiler and cook for 3–4 minutes, or until the cheese is soft and the fruit is hot. Transfer to a serving dish and serve at once.

mini pepperoni pizzas

makes twelve

BASES

1 lb 3 oz/525 g self-rising flour, plus
  extra for dusting

1 tsp salt

3 oz/85 g butter, diced

1¼–1½ cups milk

olive oil, for oiling

PEPPERONI TOPPING

¾ cup ready-made tomato
  pizza sauce

4 oz/115 g rindless smoked
  bacon, diced

1 orange bell pepper, seeded
  and chopped

3 oz/85 g pepperoni sausage, sliced

2 oz/55 g mozzarella cheese, grated

½ tsp dried oregano

olive oil, for drizzling

salt and pepper

1 Preheat the oven to 400°F/
200°C. To make the bases, sift the
flour and salt into a bowl, add the
butter, and rub in with your fingertips
until the mixture resembles bread
crumbs. Make a well in the center of
the mixture and add 1¼ cups of the
milk. Mix with the blade of a knife to a
soft dough, adding the remaining milk
if necessary.

2 Turn out onto a lightly floured
counter and knead gently. Divide
the dough into 12 equal pieces and roll
out each piece into a circle. Place on a
lightly oiled baking sheet and gently
push up the edges of each pizza to
form a rim.

3 For the topping, spread the
tomato sauce over the bases
almost to the edge. Arrange the bacon,
bell pepper, and pepperoni on top and
sprinkle with the cheese. Sprinkle with
the oregano, drizzle with oil, and
season to taste with salt and pepper.

4 Bake in the preheated oven for
10–15 minutes, or until the edges
are crisp and the cheese is bubbling.
Serve at once.

muffin pizzas

makes eight

4 English muffins

½ cup ready-made tomato
 pizza sauce

2 sun-dried tomatoes in oil,
 chopped

2 oz/55 g prosciutto

2 rings canned pineapple, chopped

½ green bell pepper, seeded
 and chopped

4½ oz/125 g mozzarella cheese,
 thinly sliced

olive oil, for drizzling

salt and pepper

fresh basil leaves, to garnish

COOK'S TIP

You don't have to use plain
English muffins for your base;
whole-wheat or cheese muffins
will also make ideal pizza bases.
English muffins freeze well, so
always keep some in the freezer
for an instant pizza.

1 Preheat the broiler to medium.
Cut the English muffins in half
and toast the cut side lightly.

2 Spread the tomato sauce evenly
over the English muffins. Sprinkle
the sun-dried tomatoes on top of the
tomato sauce.

3 Cut the prosciutto into thin strips
and place on the English muffins
with the pineapple and bell pepper.

4 Carefully arrange the cheese slices
on top.

5 Drizzle a little oil over each pizza
and add salt and pepper to taste.

6 Place under the hot broiler and
cook until the cheese melts and
bubbles.

7 Serve at once, garnished with
basil leaves.

pan bagna

serves four

16-inch/40-cm long loaf of
   country bread, thicker than a
   French baguette
about 2 tbsp fruity extra virgin
   olive oil
Black or Green Olive Tapenade
   (see page 20), for spreading
   (optional)
FILLING
2 hard-cooked eggs, shelled
1¾ oz/50 g anchovies in oil, drained
½ cup flavored olives of
   your choice
lettuce or arugula leaves, rinsed and
   patted dry
about 4 plum tomatoes, sliced
7 oz/200 g canned tuna in brine,
   well drained and flaked

VARIATION

Other typical Mediterranean
fillings for a Pan Bagna include
crushed garlic, red or bell green
peppers, young fava beans,
gherkins, artichoke hearts,
Spanish onions, fresh herbs, and
pitted olives.

1 To make the filling, slice the eggs. Drain the anchovies, then cut in half lengthwise. Pit the olives and slice in half.

2 Slice the loaf in half lengthwise. Pull out about ½ inch/1 cm of the crumb from the center of each half, leaving a border all around both halves of the loaf.

3 Generously brush both halves with oil. Spread with Tapenade, if you like a strong flavor. Arrange lettuce or arugula leaves on the bottom half of the loaf.

4 Add layers of egg, tomato, olives, anchovies, and tuna, sprinkling with oil and adding lettuce or arugula leaves between the layers. Make the filling as thick as you like.

5 Place the other bread half on top and press down firmly. Wrap tightly in plastic wrap and place on a board or plate that will fit in your refrigerator. Weight it down and let chill for several hours. To serve, slice the loaf into 4 equal portions, tying with string to secure in place, if wished.

mini pizzas

serves eight

BASIC PIZZA DOUGH

2 tsp dry yeast

1 tsp sugar

about 1 cup warm water

generous 2 cups strong all-purpose
   flour, plus extra for dusting

1 tsp salt

1 tbsp olive oil, plus extra for oiling

TOPPING

2 zucchini

generous ⅓ cup strained tomatoes

2¾ oz/75 g pancetta, diced

generous ¼ cup pitted black
   olives, chopped

salt and pepper

1 tbsp mixed dried herbs

2 tbsp olive oil

1 Place the yeast and sugar in a pitcher and mix with 4 tablespoons of the water. Set the yeast mixture aside in a warm place for 15 minutes, or until frothy.

2 Mix the flour with the salt in a large mixing bowl and make a well in the center. Add the oil, the yeast mixture, and the remaining water. Using a wooden spoon, mix together to form a smooth dough.

3 Turn the dough out onto a floured counter. Knead for 4–5 minutes, or until smooth. Return the dough to the bowl, cover with an oiled sheet of plastic wrap, and let rise for 30 minutes, or until the dough has doubled in size.

4 Preheat the oven to 400°F/200°C. Knead the dough for 2 minutes. Divide into 8 balls (or 16 balls for cocktail pizzas). Roll out each portion thinly to form circles, then carefully transfer them to an oiled baking sheet, pushing out the edges until even. The dough should be no more than ¼ inch/5 mm thick because it will rise during cooking.

5 To make the topping, finely grate the zucchini. Cover with paper towels and let stand for 10 minutes to absorb some of the juices.

6 Spread the strained tomatoes over the pizza bases and top each with the zucchini, pancetta, and olives. Season to taste with pepper, sprinkle with herbs, and drizzle with oil.

7 Bake in the preheated oven for 15 minutes, or until crisp. Season to taste with salt and pepper before serving hot.

mini pita pizzas

makes sixteen

8 thin asparagus spears

16 mini pita breads

about 6 tbsp ready-made tomato
    pizza sauce

1 oz/25 g mild Cheddar
    cheese, grated

⅛ cup ricotta cheese

2¼ oz/60 g smoked salmon

olive oil, for drizzling

pepper

fresh flatleaf parsley sprigs,
    to garnish

VARIATION

Look out for packs of smoked
salmon trimmings, which are
relatively inexpensive. Use
smoked trout in place of smoked
salmon or try experimenting with
other smoked fish, such as
smoked mackerel, with its
strong, distinctive flavor, for
a little variety.

1 Preheat the oven to 400°F/
200°C. Cut the asparagus spears
into 1-inch/2.5-cm lengths, then cut
each piece in half lengthwise.

2 Blanch the asparagus in a pan of
boiling water for 1 minute. Drain
the asparagus, plunge into cold water,
and drain again.

3 Place the pita breads on 2 baking
sheets. Spread about 1 teaspoon
of tomato pizza sauce on each pita.

4 Mix the cheeses together and
divide between the 16 pitas.

5 Cut the smoked salmon into
16 long, thin strips. Arrange
1 strip on each pita and add the
asparagus spears.

6 Drizzle over a little oil and season
to taste with pepper.

7 Bake in the preheated oven for
8–10 minutes. Garnish with
parsley sprigs and serve.

miniature onion pizzas

serves four

¾ cup strong white bread flour, plus
   flour for kneading

½ tsp active dry yeast

½ tsp salt

1 tbsp olive oil

½–1 cup warm water

TOPPING

4 tbsp olive oil

1 large onion, thinly sliced

1 tsp brown sugar

1 tsp balsamic vinegar

2 oz/55 g feta (drained weight),
   mozzarella or Gorgonzola
   cheese, grated or sliced

1 Mix the flour, yeast, and salt together in a large mixing bowl. Drizzle over half the oil. Make a well in the flour and pour in enough water to mix to a firm ball of dough. Turn out onto a floured counter and knead until it is no longer sticky. Add more flour if necessary. Grease the bowl with the remaining oil. Return the dough to the bowl, turning once to coat in the oil. Cover with a clean dish towel and let rise for 1 hour.

2 Heat the oil for the topping in a skillet over medium heat. Add the onion and cook for 10 minutes. Sprinkle with sugar and cook for an additional 5 minutes, stirring occasionally. Add the vinegar and cook for an additional 5 minutes. Remove from the heat and let cool.

3 Preheat the oven to 425°F/ 220°C. When the dough has doubled in size, knock it back and knead until smooth. Divide into quarters and roll out into thin circles. Place the dough on a baking sheet, spread with the onion, and top with cheese. Bake in the preheated oven for 10 minutes. Remove from the oven and serve.

mini artichoke pizzas

makes twelve

BASES

1 lb 3 oz/525 g self-rising flour, plus
  extra for dusting

1 tsp salt

3 oz/85 g butter, diced

1¼–1½ cups milk

olive oil, for oiling

ARTICHOKE TOPPING

¾ cup ready-made tomato
  pizza sauce

2 oz/55 g Gorgonzola cheese, sliced

4 oz/115 g canned artichoke hearts
  in oil, drained and sliced

2 shallots, chopped

2 oz/55 g Gruyère cheese, grated

4 tbsp freshly grated
  Parmesan cheese

½ tsp dried oregano

olive oil, for drizzling

salt and pepper

1 Preheat the oven to 400°F/200°C. To prepare the bases, follow Steps 1 and 2 on page 222.

2 For the topping, spread the tomato sauce over the bases almost to the edge. Arrange the Gorgonzola slices, artichoke hearts, and shallots on top. Mix the Gruyère and Parmesan together in a bowl and sprinkle over the pizzas. Sprinkle with the oregano, drizzle with oil, and season to taste with salt and pepper.

3 Bake in the preheated oven for 10–15 minutes, or until the edges are crisp and the cheese is bubbling. Serve at once.

crostini alla fiorentina

serves four

3 tbsp olive oil

1 onion, chopped

1 celery stalk, chopped

1 carrot, chopped

1–2 garlic cloves, crushed

4½ oz/125 g chicken livers

4½ oz/125 g calf's, lamb's, or
   pig's liver

⅔ cup red wine

1 tbsp tomato paste

2 tbsp chopped fresh parsley

3–4 canned anchovies, finely
   chopped

2 tbsp stock or water

salt and pepper

2–3 tbsp butter

1 tbsp capers

chopped fresh parsley, to garnish

small slices of crusty bread, toasted,
   to serve

1 Heat the oil in a skillet, add the onion, celery, carrot, and garlic, and cook gently for 4–5 minutes, or until the onion is soft but not colored.

2 Meanwhile, rinse and dry the chicken livers. Dry the calf's liver or other liver, and slice into strips. Add all the liver to the skillet and cook gently for a few minutes, until the strips are well sealed on all sides.

3 Add half of the wine and cook until it has mostly evaporated. Then add the rest of the wine, with the tomato paste, half of the parsley, the anchovies, the stock or water, a little salt, and plenty of black pepper.

4 Cover the skillet and let simmer, stirring occasionally, for about 15–20 minutes, or until tender and most of the liquid has been absorbed.

5 Let the mixture cool a little, then either coarsely grind or put into a food processor and process to a chunky purée.

6 Return to the skillet and add the butter, capers, and remaining parsley. Heat through gently until the butter melts. Adjust the seasoning and turn out into a bowl. Serve warm or cold spread on the slices of toasted crusty bread and sprinkled with chopped parsley.

filled croustades

makes forty-eight

CROUSTADES

1 lb 5 oz/600 g butter

12 large slices white bread

CHEESE & TOMATO FILLING

Tapenade (see page 233)

mozzarella cheese, thinly sliced

cherry tomatoes, halved

fresh basil leaves, to garnish

CRAB SALAD FILLING

4 oz/115 g crabmeat, drained if
    canned and thawed if frozen

½ cup mayonnaise

pinch of celery salt

2 hard-cooked eggs

fresh dill sprigs, to garnish

1 Preheat the oven to 350°F/180°C. Make the croustades in 4 batches. Melt one-quarter of the butter in a heavy-bottom pan over low heat. Meanwhile, cut out 12 circles of bread with a 3-inch/7.5-cm fluted cutter. When the butter has melted, remove the pan from the heat. Dip the bread circles into the melted butter and press them firmly into the cups of a bun pan.

2 Place a second bun pan on top to keep the bread circles in shape. Bake in the preheated oven for 15–20 minutes, or until the croustades are crisp and firm. Transfer to a wire rack to cool completely while you cook the remaining batches. When the croustades are cold, fill with your chosen filling, and serve.

3 For the Cheese & Tomato Filling, spoon Tapenade into the croustades, top each one with a slice of mozzarella and a tomato half, and garnish with a basil leaf.

4 For the Crab Salad Filling, place the crabmeat in a bowl and flake with a fork. Stir in the mayonnaise and celery salt. Shell the eggs, finely chop, and stir into the filling mixture. Spoon into the croustades and garnish with dill sprigs.

egg & tapenade toasties

makes eight

1 small French baguette

4 tomatoes, thinly sliced

4 hard-cooked eggs

4 bottled or canned anchovies in
olive oil, drained and halved
lengthwise

8 marinated pitted black olives

few fine frisée leaves, to garnish

TAPENADE

½ cup pitted black olives

6 bottled or canned anchovies in
olive oil, drained

2 tbsp capers, rinsed

2 garlic cloves, coarsely chopped

1 tsp Dijon mustard

2 tbsp lemon juice

1 tsp fresh thyme leaves

pepper

4–5 tbsp olive oil

1 For the Tapenade, place the olives, anchovies, capers, garlic, mustard, lemon juice, thyme, and pepper to taste in a food processor and process for 20–25 seconds, or until smooth. Scrape down the sides of the mixing bowl. With the motor running, gradually add the oil through the feeder tube to make a smooth paste. Spoon the paste into a bowl, cover with plastic wrap, and set aside until required.

2 Preheat the broiler to medium. Cut the baguette into 8 slices, discarding the crusty ends. Toast on both sides under the hot broiler until light golden brown. Let cool.

3 To assemble the toasties, spread a little of the Tapenade on 1 side of each slice of toast. Top with the tomato slices. Shell the eggs, then slice and arrange over the tomatoes. Dot a little of the remaining Tapenade on each egg slice. Wind the anchovies around the egg slices in an "S" shape. Halve the marinated olives and arrange 2 halves on each toasty. Garnish with the frisée leaves and serve.

mozzarella snack

serves four

8 slices bread, preferably slightly
stale, crusts removed

3½ oz/100 g mozzarella cheese,
thickly sliced

generous ¼ cup black olives,
chopped

8 canned anchovies, drained and
chopped

16 fresh basil leaves

salt and pepper

4 eggs, beaten

⅔ cup milk

oil, for deep-frying

fresh basil sprigs, to garnish

1 Using a sharp knife, cut each slice of bread into 2 triangles. Top 8 of the bread triangles with the mozzarella slices, olives, and anchovies.

2 Place the basil leaves on top and season to taste with salt and pepper.

3 Lay the other 8 triangles of bread over the top and press down round the edges to seal.

4 Mix the eggs and milk together and pour into an ovenproof dish. Add the sandwiches and let them soak for about 5 minutes.

5 Heat the oil in a deep-fat fryer or large pan to 350–375°F/ 180–190°C, or until a cube of bread browns in 30 seconds.

6 Before cooking the sandwiches, press the edges together again.

7 Carefully place the sandwiches in the oil and deep-fry, turning once, for 2 minutes, or until golden. Remove the sandwiches with a slotted spoon and drain on paper towels. Garnish with basil and serve at once.

basil zucchini toasties

serves four

4 slices white bread

2 oz/55 g butter, melted

4 eggs

2 cups milk

1 small onion, finely chopped

1 zucchini, grated

1 cup grated cheese

2 cups fresh bread crumbs

1 tbsp finely chopped fresh basil

salt and pepper

pinch of paprika

2 tbsp grated Parmesan cheese

1 Preheat the oven to 375°F/
190°C. Remove the crusts from
the bread and press them into the cups
of a muffin pan. Brush well with
melted butter.

2 Beat the eggs well in a mixing
bowl. Stir in the milk. Add the
onion, zucchini, cheese, bread crumbs,
basil, and salt and pepper to taste.
Mix well.

3 Carefully pour the egg mixture
into the bread cases. Sprinkle
with the paprika and Parmesan cheese.
Bake in the preheated oven for
45 minutes, or until set and golden.

4 Turn off the oven, but leave the
toasties in the oven to cool for
10 minutes before transferring to a
serving platter.

sincronizadas

serves six

vegetable oil, for oiling

about 10 flour tortillas

about 1 lb 2 oz/500 g grated cheese

8 oz/225 g cooked ham, diced

salsa of choice

sour cream sprinkled with chopped
   fresh herbs, to serve

VARIATION

For a vegetarian version, cook
8 oz/225 g thinly sliced
mushrooms in a little olive oil
with a crushed garlic clove and
use instead of the ham.
Alternatively, lightly sauté finely
chopped garlic in a little oil, then
add rinsed spinach leaves and
cook until wilted; chop and
substitute for the ham.

COOK'S TIP

Protect your hands with oven
mitts when turning the tortillas
out onto the plate.

1 Lightly oil a nonstick skillet. Off
the heat, place 1 tortilla in the
skillet and top with a layer of cheese
and ham. Generously spread salsa over
another tortilla and place, salsa-side
down, on top of the cheese and ham
tortilla in the skillet.

2 Place over medium heat
and cook until the cheese is
melted and the base of the tortilla is
golden brown.

3 Place a heatproof plate, upside-
down, on top of the skillet. Taking
care to protect your hands, hold the
plate firmly in place and carefully invert
the skillet to turn the "sandwich" out
onto the plate.

4 Slide the "sandwich" back
into the skillet and cook
until the underside of the tortilla is
golden brown.

5 Remove from the skillet and
serve, cut into wedges, with sour
cream sprinkled with herbs. Repeat
with the remaining ingredients.

mini focaccia

serves four

2 tbsp olive oil, plus extra for oiling

2¼ cups strong white flour, plus
  extra for dusting

½ tsp salt

1 sachet active dry yeast

generous 1 cup lukewarm water

½ cup pitted green or black olives,
  halved

TOPPING

2 red onions, sliced

2 tbsp olive oil

1 tsp sea salt

1 tbsp fresh thyme leaves

1 Oil several baking sheets. Sift the flour and salt into a bowl, stir in the yeast, pour in the oil and water, and mix to form a dough.

2 Turn the dough out onto a lightly floured counter and knead for 5 minutes. Alternatively, use an electric mixer with a dough hook.

3 Place the dough in an oiled bowl, cover, and leave in a warm place for 1–1½ hours, or until doubled in size. Knock back the dough by kneading it again for 1–2 minutes.

4 Knead half the olives into the dough. Divide the dough into quarters and shape the quarters into circles. Place them on the baking sheets and push your fingers into the dough to create a dimpled effect.

5 To make the topping, sprinkle the onions and remaining olives over the circles. Drizzle the oil over the top and sprinkle with the sea salt and thyme leaves. Cover and let stand for 30 minutes.

6 Preheat the oven to 375°F/ 190°C. Bake for 20–25 minutes, or until the focaccia are golden. Transfer to a wire rack and let cool before serving.

VARIATION

Use this quantity of dough
to make 1 large focaccia,
if you prefer.

sun-dried tomato rolls

serves eight

3½ oz/100 g butter, melted and
   cooled slightly, plus extra
   for greasing

1½ cups strong white bread flour,
   plus extra for dusting

½ tsp salt

1 sachet active dry yeast

3 tbsp milk, warmed, plus extra
   for brushing

2 eggs, beaten

scant ¼ cup sun-dried tomatoes,
   well drained and finely chopped

1 Lightly grease a baking sheet. Sift
the flour and salt into a large
bowl. Stir in the yeast, then pour in the
butter, milk, and eggs. Mix together to
form a dough.

2 Turn the dough out onto a floured
counter and knead for 5 minutes.
Alternatively, use an electric mixer with
a dough hook.

3 Place the dough in a greased
bowl, cover, and let rise in a
warm place for 1–1½ hours, or until
doubled in size. Knock back the dough
by kneading for 2–3 minutes.

4 Preheat the oven to 450°F/
230°C. Knead the sun-dried
tomatoes into the dough, sprinkling
the counter with a little extra flour
because the tomatoes are quite oily.
Divide the dough into 8 equal-size
balls and place them on the baking
sheet. Cover and let stand for
30 minutes, or until doubled in size.

5 Brush the rolls with milk and bake
in the preheated oven for
10–15 minutes, or until golden brown.
Transfer the rolls to a wire rack and let
cool slightly before serving.

VARIATION

Add some finely chopped
anchovies or olives to the
dough in Step 4 for extra flavor,
if you like.

239

cheese & chive bread

serves eight

2 tbsp butter, melted, plus extra
   for greasing

1½ cups self-rising flour

1 tsp salt

1 tsp mustard powder

3½ oz/100 g sharp cheese, grated

2 tbsp snipped fresh chives

1 egg, beaten

⅔ cup milk

1 Preheat the oven to 375°F/
190°C. Grease a 9-inch/23-cm
square cake pan with a little butter
and line the bottom of the pan with
parchment paper.

2 Sift the flour, salt, and mustard
powder into a large bowl.
Reserve 3 tablespoons of the cheese
for sprinkling, then stir the remaining
cheese into the bowl with the chives.
Mix together well. Add the egg, butter,
and milk to the dry ingredients and stir
thoroughly to combine.

COOK'S TIP

You can use any hard sharp
cheese of your choice for this
recipe, such as Cheddar,
Cheshire, or Leicester.

3 Spoon the mixture into the pan
and spread with a knife. Sprinkle
over the reserved cheese.

4 Bake in the preheated oven for
30 minutes. Let the bread cool
slightly in the pan. Turn out onto a
wire rack to cool completely. Cut into
triangles to serve.

olive cake

makes twelve–fifteen slices

butter, for greasing

1½ cups pitted black or
   green olives, or a mixture

scant 2 cups self-rising flour

4 large eggs

1 tbsp superfine sugar

salt and pepper

½ cup milk

½ cup olive oil

COOK'S TIP

The Olive Cake will keep fresh for
up to 2 days if stored in an
airtight container.

---

1 Preheat the oven to 400°F/200°C. Lightly grease an 8-inch/20-cm cake pan, 2 inches/5 cm deep. Line the bottom with parchment paper cut to fit. Put the olives in a small bowl and toss in 2 tablespoons of the flour.

2 Break the eggs into a large bowl and lightly whisk. Stir in the sugar and salt and pepper to taste. Stir in the milk and oil.

3 Sift the remaining flour into the bowl, add the coated olives, and stir together. Spoon the mixture into the prepared pan and smooth the surface with a knife.

4 Bake in the preheated oven for 45 minutes. Reduce the oven temperature to 325°F/160°C and bake for an additional 15 minutes, or until the cake is risen, golden, and coming away from the side of the pan.

5 Remove from the oven and let cool in the pan on a wire rack for 20 minutes. Remove from the pan, peel off the lining paper, and let cool completely. Store the cake in an airtight container.

specialty bread chips

serves four

4 pita breads or bagels

2 tbsp olive oil or melted butter

TOPPINGS

1 tsp black onion, dill, cumin, or
   crushed coriander seeds
   (optional)

1 tsp chopped fresh rosemary
   (optional)

1 tsp sea salt (optional)

2 garlic cloves, finely chopped
   (optional)

1 Preheat the oven to 400°F/
200°C. Cut the pita breads or
bagels in half horizontally.

2 Brush the pita breads or bagels
with oil or butter.

3 Arrange the bread on a baking
sheet and sprinkle with whichever
toppings you have decided to use.
Heat in the preheated oven for
5 minutes, or until crisp and golden.
Remove from the oven, cut into fingers
or triangles, and serve at once
with a selection of dips and spreads
(see pages 10–55).

goat cheese & chive croutons

serves four

½ cup extra virgin olive oil

8 x ½-inch/1-cm thick slices French
   baguette or ciabatta

4 oz/115 g goat cheese

pepper

1 tbsp finely snipped fresh chives

1 Preheat the oven to 350°F/
180°C. Pour the oil into a shallow
dish and place the bread in it. Let
stand for 1–2 minutes, then turn and
leave for an additional 2 minutes. The
bread should be thoroughly saturated
in oil.

2 Meanwhile, if the cheese has
come in a log, cut into 8 slices.
If the cheese has come in circles,
crumble coarsely.

3 Place the bread on a baking sheet
and bake in the preheated oven
for 5 minutes. Remove the sheet from
the oven, turn the bread over, and top
each slice with cheese. Sprinkle
generously with pepper.

4 Return the sheet to the oven
for an additional 5 minutes to
heat the cheese thoroughly. Remove
from the oven, arrange the croutons on
plates and sprinkle with chives.
Serve at once.

sesame bread sticks

makes thirty-two

1½ cups unbleached strong bread
  flour, plus extra for dusting

1¾ cups strong whole-wheat flour

1 sachet active dry yeast

2 tsp salt

½ tsp sugar

about 2 cups lukewarm water

4 tbsp olive oil, plus extra for oiling

1 egg white, lightly beaten

sesame seeds, for sprinkling

1 Combine the flours, yeast, salt, and sugar in a bowl and make a well in the center. Gradually stir in most of the water and all the oil, to make a dough. Gradually add the remaining water, if necessary, drawing in all the flour.

2 Turn out onto a lightly floured counter and knead the dough for 10 minutes, or until smooth and elastic. Wash the bowl and lightly coat with oil.

3 Shape the dough into a ball and place in the bowl, turning once to coat in the oil. Cover tightly with a clean dish towel or lightly oiled plastic wrap and set aside in a warm place until the dough has doubled in size.

4 Preheat the oven to 450°F/ 230°C. Line a baking sheet with parchment paper. Turn out the dough onto a lightly floured counter and knead lightly. Divide in half. Roll each piece into a 16-inch/40-cm rope, then cut each rope into 8 equal pieces. Cut each piece in half again to make a total of 32 pieces.

5 Keep the dough that you are not working with covered with a clean dish towel or plastic wrap to prevent it drying out. Roll each piece of dough into a thin 10-inch/25-cm rope on a very lightly floured counter. Carefully transfer to the baking sheet.

6 Cover and set aside to rise for 10 minutes. Brush with egg white, then sprinkle evenly and thickly with sesame seeds. Bake in the preheated oven for 10 minutes.

7 Brush again with egg white and bake for 5 minutes, or until golden brown and crisp. Transfer the bread sticks to wire racks to cool.

cheese straws

makes sixty

1½ cups all-purpose flour, plus
     extra for dusting

salt and pepper

cayenne pepper

mustard powder

4 oz/115 g butter, diced, plus extra
     for greasing

¾ cup freshly grated Parmesan or
     romano cheese

2 egg yolks

1–2 tbsp cold water (optional)

1 egg white, lightly beaten, to glaze

1 Sift the flour into a bowl with a pinch each of salt, pepper, cayenne pepper, and mustard powder. Add the butter and rub in with your fingertips until the mixture resembles bread crumbs. Stir in the cheese. Add the egg yolks and mix well, adding a little of the cold water, as required, to bind. Shape the dough into a ball.

2 Preheat the oven to 425°F/ 220°C. Grease several baking sheets. Roll out the dough on a lightly floured counter to about ½ inch/1 cm thick. Using a sharp knife, cut into fingers and arrange on the baking sheets, spaced slightly apart. Brush with egg white.

3 Bake in the preheated oven for 8–10 minutes, or until golden brown. Remove from the oven and let cool on the baking sheets. When completely cool, store in an airtight container, but they are best served as fresh as possible.

garlic & chive cookies

makes twenty-five

2 oz/55 g unsalted butter, softened,
plus extra for greasing

2 tbsp finely snipped fresh chives

scant 1 cup all-purpose flour, plus
extra for dusting

2 tbsp freshly grated
Parmesan cheese

1 egg yolk

2–3 tbsp ice water

3 garlic cloves, finely chopped

1 egg yolk, beaten, to glaze

1 Using a wooden spoon or a fork, beat the butter with the snipped fresh chives in a mixing bowl until thoroughly combined.

2 Sift the flour into a bowl and stir in the Parmesan. Add the chive butter and rub in with your fingertips until the mixture resembles bread crumbs. Add the egg yolk and enough of the water to make a soft dough. Shape the dough into a ball, wrap in foil, and let chill in the refrigerator for 30 minutes.

3 Preheat the oven to 400°F/200°C. Grease a baking sheet with a little butter. Unwrap the dough and roll out on a lightly floured counter. Sprinkle the garlic evenly over the dough, then fold it in half and roll out thinly again. Cut out circles using a 2½-inch/6-cm fluted cutter.

4 Place the circles on the baking sheet and brush with the beaten egg to glaze. Bake in the preheated oven for 15–20 minutes, or until golden. Remove from the oven and let cool for a few minutes. Transfer to a wire rack to cool completely. Store in an airtight container until required.

ham & parmesan pinwheels

serves four

1 small loaf of bread

4 tbsp butter, mustard, or
   cream cheese

4 slices of ham

4 tbsp grated Parmesan cheese

8 sun-dried tomatoes (optional)

VARIATION

You can use any variety of
ham—honey-roasted, cured, or
smoked. Alternatively, use slices
of smoked salmon with
cream cheese.

---

1 Preheat the oven to 350°F/
180°C. Grease a baking sheet.
Remove the crusts from the bread and
cut into 4 slices lengthwise. Place each
slice between 2 pieces of waxed paper
and flatten with a rolling pin. Remove
the paper.

2 Spread each slice of bread with
butter, mustard, or cream cheese
and top with slices of ham. Sprinkle
Parmesan cheese over the top. If you
are using sun-dried tomatoes, chop
them and sprinkle over the cheese.

3 Roll up the bread along its length,
then cut into ½-inch/1-cm slices
crosswise. Place the pinwheels,
cut-side up, on the baking sheet. Bake
in the preheated oven for 5 minutes,
or until the cheese has melted. Remove
from the oven, spear each with a
cocktail stick and serve hot or cold.

anchovy bites

makes thirty

generous 1 cup all-purpose flour,
  plus extra for dusting

3 oz/85 g butter, cut into
  small pieces

4 tbsp freshly grated
  Parmesan cheese

salt and pepper

2–3 tbsp cold water

3 tbsp Dijon mustard

ANCHOIADE

4 oz/115 g canned anchovies
  in olive oil, drained

generous ⅓ cup milk

2 garlic cloves, coarsely chopped

1 tbsp chopped fresh
  flatleaf parsley

1 tbsp chopped fresh basil

1 tbsp lemon juice

2 tbsp blanched almonds, toasted
  and coarsely chopped

4 tbsp olive oil

pepper

1 To make the dough, sift the flour into a large bowl. Add the butter and rub in with your fingertips until the mixture resembles bread crumbs. Stir in half the Parmesan cheese and salt. Add enough cold water to form a firm dough. Knead briefly, wrap in plastic wrap and let chill in the refrigerator for 30 minutes.

2 Meanwhile, make the anchoiade. Put the anchovies into a small bowl and pour over the milk. Let soak for 10 minutes. Drain the anchovies and pat dry on paper towels. Discard the milk.

3 Coarsely chop the anchovies and put into a food processor with the garlic, parsley, basil, lemon juice, almonds, and 2 tablespoons of the oil. Process until smooth, then transfer to a bowl and stir in the remaining oil and pepper to taste. Set aside.

4 Preheat the oven to 400°F/200°C. Remove the dough from the refrigerator and roll out very thinly on a lightly floured counter to a rectangle measuring 20 x 15 inches/50 x 38 cm. Spread thinly with 2 tablespoons of the anchoiade and the mustard. Sprinkle over the remaining Parmesan cheese and pepper to taste.

5 Starting from a long edge, roll up tightly, then slice the roll crosswise into ½-inch/1-cm thick slices. Arrange cut-side up and well spaced on a nonstick baking sheet.

6 Cook in the preheated oven for 20 minutes, or until golden. Let cool on a wire rack.

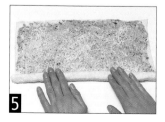